Humble and Awake

Humble and Awake:
Coping with our Comatose Culture

by
Thomas G. Casey, S.J.

Templegate Publishers
Springfield, Illinois

First published in 2004 by
Templegate Publishers
302 East Adams Street
P.O. Box 5152
Springfield, Illinois 62705-5152
217-522-3353
templegate.com

ISBN 0-87243-265-3
Library of Congress Control Number 2004112933

Cover: William Blake's *Dante and Statius Sleep While Virgil Watches* from
The Divine Comedy

Dedication

To my father and mother, Michael and Mary,
My sisters Anne-Marie and Michelle,
My brother Paul and my brother-in-law Michael

Contents

Acknowledgements   9

Introduction   11

Chapter 1: Glimpses of Humility   17

Chapter 2: How the Coma Began   35

Chapter 3: False Hope   51

Chapter 4: Signs of Wakefulness   67

Chapter 5: A Secular Wake-up Call   85

Chapter 6: The Face that Wakes Us Up   95

Chapter 7: Alive or Comatose—John or Judas?   109

Chapter 8: Wake Up, Sleeping Beauty!   139

Chapter 9: Responsibility for All   149

Chapter 10: Living Humility with Hope
            in Holy Week   165

Epilogue   189

Notes   193

Bibliography   203

Index   205

Acknowledgements

We Irish are justly famous for the many world-class authors we have produced. But a less well-known fact is the enormous number of *potential* writers who are liberally sprinkled throughout the country. For the truth is that in Ireland a lot of books never get written in the first place. They spill out conversationally in the convivial surroundings of the local pub. This could easily have happened in my case. I could have ended up waxing eloquently about humility and wakefulness, throwing out all sorts of interesting ideas and never really following any of them up. But things changed when I was recently reassigned to Rome. In one of those frequent ironies of life, I now find I have more time to think and write, although I am living in the midst of a people that has elevated conversation to the level of a fine art.

Writing about a topic like humility has brought me up against my own distinct lack of it. Therefore I am especially grateful to the countless people, starting with my parents and family, to whom I owe whatever glimmers of goodness are reflected in the pages you are about to read. A big thank you to Cecilia, John, Iggy, Az, Joe and especially Mary, who have been there both when I needed them and when I forgot that I did.

Finally thank you to Fr. Gerald O'Collins, S.J., who with his boyish and winning enthusiasm, encouraged me to sit down and write this book in the first place.

Introduction

Angels can fly because they can take themselves lightly.

Gilbert Keith Chesterton, Orthodoxy

During a coma, the brain is at its lowest level of performance; if it sinks any deeper, the person dies. Outwardly a coma is similar to sleep, but at least the sleeping person can regain relative or full alertness in a matter of seconds. The person in a coma, on the other hand, is unable to respond to any external stimuli. It is distressing to sit long hours at the bedside of someone whose eyes are wide open but whose stare is vacant, who merely survives but is robbed of the exhilaration of life.

If injuries to the brain cause actual comas, then comas in the figurative sense of the word that I am using here are brought about by injuries to the soul. The soul is hurt when the person no longer acts rightly and so they become deaf to the call of goodness and their capacity to love is steadily eroded. And I believe that the soul of our culture has been wounded today. It does not follow that everyone in our culture is in a spiritual coma; thankfully there are many people of deep goodness around us. But for all that, this book is not an unqualified celebration of our world. Although a comatose culture does not necessarily throw everyone into a coma, it undoubtedly makes it more difficult to remain spiritually alert and alive.

Our culture continues to be drawn by truth, goodness and beauty; indeed it would no longer be a human culture if it were not attracted to these gems. But our culture simultaneously undermines them in practice. This is a somewhat dramatic way of saying that our culture is not perfect. To use an environmental metaphor, our cultural air is no longer pure. For each of us there is the danger of becoming so inured to our polluted cultural ambience that we end up persuading ourselves that we are in fact inhaling fresh air. It is a double tragedy to suffer the inexorable onslaught of sickness all the while believing that you are in the best of health: disease is then further aggravated by ignorance. A diagnosis of our illness is needed.

We are at a crucial moment in world history. We are in a kind of "Holy Week," analogous to the final week of Jesus' earthly life, a period of unease and contrasting moods of light and darkness that precedes the resurrection. But although God will come again soon, it is vital to stress that God's "soon" is not our soon, and so our business is not to speculate uselessly about the future but to uncover the hidden drama of the present, to discern how God is speaking to us in the here and now, which is the time of salvation. Rather than fixating on an apocalyptic vision of the future, it is vital to see how God is already communicating to us in the signs of the times. He is speaking through humble old men and women, through poor people who have never received schooling, through the meek who have never appeared on the covers of celebrity magazines or on prime-time television. These are the true prophets, priests and kings of our time, through whose neglected voices the King of Glory speaks. I hope this book can encourage us to join their ranks.

Humility is of the utmost importance for a comatose culture. First of all, it takes humility to recognize that we are in a quagmire; secondly, it takes humility to realize that we only sink deeper into quicksand the more we try to get out through our own unaided efforts. The only way to rise from the morass is by accepting help. Being humble means recognizing that we cannot do it on our own, but we can do everything with God's help.

The prospect of plumbing the depths of humility is itself enough to induce a sinking feeling. This feeling is only intensified when the "plumber" in question happens to be a Jesuit. The very thought of a Jesuit exploring the virtue of humility is bound to raise a few chuckles, if not elicit downright disbelief. After all, it is not a virtue for which we are noted. Despite the fact that Ignatius of Loyola famously called the Society of Jesus "this least Company," the phrase tends to be used with undisguised irony, above all by Jesuits. If I can offer any credible reason for writing this book, it is the fact that I need to learn more about humility and put it into practice. In case I forget how far I have to go, the following anecdote helps me keep my feet on the ground: shortly after his birth the child Jesus wakes up in his manger at Bethlehem, only to see an ox and an ass standing next to him with moronic expressions on their faces. "So this is the Company of Jesus," he sighs.

Humility is about keeping one's feet on the ground; it is earthy, in accord with the root meaning of the word. But it can easily evanesce like some precious incense into a gilded cloud of unknowing. In an effort to keep humility down to earth, I will engage in a dialogue with both Western religious and humanistic thought, while appealing to the wisdom of several prophetic figures. The most important of these is the apostle John, the disciple closest to Jesus. Then there is Fyodor Dostoevsky (1821-1881), the uncompromising and apocalyptic Russian novelist, who is unrivaled in his searing depictions of the human condition. I will draw from Hans Urs von Balthasar (1905-1988), whose theology, with its innovative use of beauty and drama, is as fascinating as it is seductive. And I will turn repeatedly to the Jewish philosopher Emmanuel Levinas (1906-1995), whose life experience so undermined his faith in Western culture that he sought to rouse humanity from its torpor so that it would not descend into barbarism yet again. Although I do not devote any specific chapter to the practice and teaching of Jesus on humility, every chapter will have something to say about him.

I draw on a rich and living Christian tradition by appealing to John, von Balthasar, and Dostoevsky. By turning to Levinas' thought, which invites us to respond to the graced mystery of other people in a more alert way, I draw on Jewish wisdom which has enriched Christianity in so many ways. Levinas' philosophy is difficult to categorize. He would be glad to hear this, since his most insistent complaint about Western philosophy is that it tries to grasp whatever is different all too easily. Born in Lithuania, an adopted Frenchman, he did not fit easily into French philosophy. Levinas was never as trend-driven as many postmodernists and refused to modify his philosophy for the sake of changing philosophical fashions. Now his thought is decidedly hip. Although thirty years ago he might have been dismissed as anachronistic and out-of-date, he was hailed as a prophetic figure by the time of his death on

Christmas Day 1995. Which goes to show how much some of his fellow philosophers are slaves to fashion!

The three principal inspirations behind Levinas' thought are Jewish tradition, the great nineteenth-century Russian novels, and the phenomenological movement, a current in twentieth century philosophy that focused on the world understood as a lived experience before it is made into an object of theoretical knowledge. Despite the subtleties and shifting complexities of this triple influence, the heart of Levinas' thought is radically simple. He challenges us to wake up to the other person, to respond in loving service. Levinas likes to use the term "other" to stipulate that the other is essentially unknown and unknowable.

This book is written with energy and urgency not only because I am impassioned about waking up but more especially because I am irresistibly attracted by God. In this book I have chosen many stories and characters that inspire me to emulation. The face of Jesus endlessly fascinates me, and is gradually transforming my life. The story of Adam and Eve teaches me a lesson I do not apply often enough: how to recognize temptation and how to cope with it. I am astonished at John the Evangelist because of the greatness of his love and the greatness of the One he loved. Because John is so vital and alive for me, I feel a little closer to his best friend—Jesus. Dostoevsky's passion for God reveals my own to be as thin and flimsy as lace. As for beauty, I could not live without it. Christianity without beauty is infinitely worse than Christmas without Santa Claus or Ireland without sun. At least you grow accustomed to the latter deprivations. And finally it is because of John the Evangelist that I believe we have entered a period analogous to the final week of Jesus' earthly life.[1] I will explain what I mean by this at greater length in the final chapter. Let me say for now that we are at a decisive moment in world history. Of course there is no telling how long our particular "Holy Week" will last. It might linger on for decades, centuries, or longer. John, the apostle who talked most about the End Times, was apparently also the apostle who had the longest life of the twelve. For all his talk of the end of the world he did not rush towards Armageddon on a rabid roller-coaster ride. Rather he "abided" in many senses of the word. He was the most contemplative apostle, the one who stayed closest to Jesus, leaning against his heart. And that is why John's writings contain a meaning that is vaster than words. It is above all in his letters that John never tires of speaking of the most dramatic truth of all: not the scenario of the End Times but the majestic truth about the centrality and nobility of love. John reached the perfection of intelligence and wisdom because love utterly refined his spirit. Love sheltered him from evil and helped him to fly along the path of goodness. It is love that will awaken us to the mysteries that lie hidden in our midst.

1

Glimpses of Humility

It's a very unusual emotion I am feeling. I think it's called humility.

Bono of U2
at 2001 Grammy Awards in Los Angeles

Humility was traditionally cherished as a virtue that enhanced human existence, as an ingredient of a life well lived. It has rightly come under suspicion because of its association with humiliation, with negativity, and with self-hatred. Too often humility has degenerated into abject groveling and servile fawning. We squirm on meeting real-life people who remind us of characters like Dickens' wonderfully hideous Uriah Heep. His unctuous pomposity certainly makes for an entertaining fictional character, but in real life this kind of warped humility offends wisdom and common sense.

The words "humility" and "humiliation" are orthographic neighbors: open any dictionary and you will find that these words are uncomfortably close together. But much more disquieting is the often blurred border between them. This lack of clarity has various causes. For one thing, humility is relative: it can mean vastly different things for people at different levels of society. It can be relatively painless to invite a billionaire to be humble if you allow him or her to remain a billionaire. But if a person already feels humiliated because of homelessness and unemployment, there is nothing funny about telling them to be humble—this is rubbing it in. Even more alarming is the fact that people have been humiliated and stigmatized in the name of a false humility. They were abused or exploited by people who were meant to take care of them, and were then told that part of humility was to accept this appalling behavior and not ask questions. We know of horrific incidents of child abuse by priests and pastors. But in addition to these sickening individual acts, there was at times a systematic pattern of humiliating treatment in so-called Christian institutions, from a meager diet to corporal punishment to unrelenting labor. Those responsible for such an inhuman regime regarded humiliation as the inevitable price to be paid for being illegitimate, an orphan, a single mother, a child migrant, and so on—as though this harsh training in "humility" were the ransom to redeem one's soul.

It is not surprising that people are wary of humility today, given the way it has been misused in the past. However, it is not just the gross aberrations of humility that disturb us. The very idea of humility runs counter to our self-understanding as human beings who have come of age, who are only truly happy in bowing to the authority of our own experience, and are no longer comfortable submitting to institutions and traditions of questionable integrity and dubious ethics. It seems audacious to argue for a reinstatement of the discarded virtue of humility. Perhaps that is why contemporary commentators tend to be rather careful and nuanced in their appeals to it.

In *Darwin's Worms* (1999) the essayist and psychotherapist Adam Phillips, with the help of Darwin and Freud, argues for a humble approach to the inevitable fact of death. Phillips does not pretend that death is an easy fact of life; he accepts that it is a huge loss and one in which we cannot turn back the clock. Death is a particularly radical cut-off point in his view; Phillips does not believe in an afterlife. Whatever his reservations regarding immortality, Philips comes up with some thought-provoking ideas—they originate in worms.

Darwin's name is indissolubly linked to his controversial thought on evolution. But Darwin also devoted enormous patience and time to the painstaking observation of the lowly earthworm, whose behavior he watched and catalogued meticulously. Personally, I have always respected earthworms enough to sidestep them on a wet garden path, but I have never given them much thought. This is why I find Phillips' reflections so intriguing. Although I obviously do not accept the thesis of Darwin or Freud that immortality is dead, I am fascinated by Darwin's discovery of how much the humble earthworm is a source of life and nourishment for the rest of us.

Over time each earthworm swallows enormous quantities of soil. Darwin reckoned that every piece of fertile soil on the planet must have passed at least once through the bodies of earthworms. Even though we remain largely ignorant of their contribution, earthworms provide an immense and indispensable service to the well-being of land. As they burrow into the earth they swallow soil from the surface, digest it and then deposit the residue at a deeper level. On returning to the surface they bring soil from deeper down, mixing it with the topsoil. So they literally plough the land, making it more porous and aerating it. They create channels for plants to take root more easily. Their intestines secrete material that glues particles of soil together, thus retaining valuable nutrients and helping to prevent erosion. Not only do they consume manure, rubbish and organic materials; they also transform these substances into rich topsoil. We might think that the earthworms don't do much more than slither and slide a few inches along the garden lawn each day; in fact these little creatures have transformed our planet for the good over thousands upon thousands of years.

Phillips sees the sublime implications of the humble work of earthworms. The simple earthworm succeeds in doing an enormously complex job: it transforms the intricately designed and carefully balanced global ecosystem, without destroying the world or upsetting the environmental balance in the process. Its example could also have a dramatic effect on the way we think about life. The earthworm has no great plan in mind; it is not set on world revolution. It labors simply to survive, but its work has unintended consequences that make a huge difference to humanity: without the earthworm this world would not be an easy place to live in for the rest of us.

Like the earthworms, we live on an amazing planet, full of promise and potential. If we took our work in this world more seriously, we might transform this planet in unlikely and welcome ways. If we followed the example of earthworms and focused on the world before us, we too might make our environment more conducive to new life and growth. Phillips is inviting us to accept our humble status with all its immense drawbacks, above all the certain fact of death. If we accept our lowly place we may, like the earthworm, be able to dig more deeply into the riches under our noses. Through descending in humility we will ascend in happiness.[1] Phillips' ruminations make me wonder if the biblical description of being "a worm and no man" is such an abysmal state after all!

Humble people draw little attention to themselves. Yet, with a minimum of fuss, they accomplish great things. I am not suggesting that people should consider themselves worms: for too long a spineless anthropology has been unfortunately associated with Christianity. The truth is that each person is a son or daughter of God. We should only consider the "wormlike" elements in our mortal nature in conjunction with the majesty that characterizes us. It is only permissible to look on our nothingness if we simultaneously keep our greatness before our eyes. Everyone is special as Winston Churchill humorously suggested in his famous dinner party remark to Violet Asquith, "We are all worms. But I do believe I am a glow worm." Although none of us is a worm, each of us can learn a lot from their unfussy service and prodigious industry. These humble creatures have a mighty lesson to teach us.

Our dependence upon earthworms is just one instance of our many hidden and obvious debts. Yet because we are so often blind to the fact that "the world is charged with the grandeur of God," as Hopkins wrote, because we often see nature as something simply to be used, we also forget that we are dependent on the natural world. We need fresh air to breathe, pure water to drink, healthy crops to eat. And if we treat nature arrogantly, we will reap our just rewards. There are signs that the wheel is coming full circle now. The earth is no longer the hospitable host it once was. Our scientific and technological innovations have developed at such an accelerating rate that we are now beginning to worry whether they will destroy us. We have enough nuclear weapons to wipe out our civilization several times over. We have thrown away so much garbage that the whole world is littered. We already see strange climatic patterns with record heat waves and rainfalls. We see animals and plants deceived by unexpected reversals of temperature: swallows migrating prematurely, plants blooming out of season. God's act of creation was characterized by order; there is something sinister in its usurpation by disorder.

The ancient Greek philosopher Pythagoras called the universe a *cosmos*, because he marveled at its orderly, proportionate, harmonious and beautiful nature. It fitted together in an amazingly satisfying manner. But today we sometimes wonder if it has descended into *chaos*, another Greek word, this time meaning an empty, gaping void, a jarring, shapeless mess of matter. God created the world from nothing, shaping it from the formlessness of chaos into the beauty of cosmos. Unfortunately, human beings are not always alive to God's promptings and can go in a disastrous reverse direction, from cosmos back to chaos.

It is as though because we have overstepped the place allotted to us in the order of creation, the universe itself is crying out against us. It is a bizarre replay of the story of Adam and Eve: in their desire to surpass their creaturely status and equal God, they were exiled from the Garden of Eden, and the earth that once brought forth fruits for them, now only provided thorns and brambles. Their repudiation of humility unleashed a catastrophic chain of events, from Cain's murder of his brother to a world-wide flood in Noah's time.

I do not refer to Genesis by way of digression. Humility is truly cosmic in its implications, just as Adam and Eve's disobedience turned out to be. Humility is not simply an individual and private disposition. It should not be merely regarded as part of a privatized faith. It is not an obscure paragraph in a dusty treatise on moral theology. For the sake of truthfulness, for the sake of our very survival and happiness, our dependence should not be forgotten. Humility is not a superfluous remnant from an immature past; it is an essential part of a truer and more authentic future.

To help retrieve humility for the future from the wisdom of the past, I want to begin with Emmanuel Levinas. He has discerned the importance of humility. He is fond of evoking the biblical figures of the widow, the orphan, and the stranger. Is this romantic nostalgia on his part, a harking back to a world that seems all the more appealing because it can never be recaptured? Levinas' imagery, although ancient, is not out of date. He prophetically puts into question the kind of life that takes the self's rights and privileges for granted: "The question *par excellence*, or the first question, is not 'why is there being rather than nothing?' but 'have I the right to be?'"[2] This is an excellent question and not one that we are inclined to ask spontaneously of ourselves. Our instinctive reaction, especially when someone treads on our toes, is "who the hell do you think you are!" In fact, at that moment we are convinced we know what the other person is and our image of them is decidedly unflattering. Levinas takes a much more humble position vis-à-vis the other. He does not believe that the other can be comprehended at all. The other is an utter mystery. To start with the question of being, defining the other within that context ("you are a human being like me"), going from there to the question of goodness ("therefore I have a duty to act ethically toward you"), reverses the correct order. What comes first, what is most important, is not the fact that I am but the fact that I find myself faced with someone who calls me to respond. It is an intriguing and disconcerting reversal.

In Christianity the wisdom of ethics precedes the science of being (ontology): followers of Jesus are called to act justly before they even exist! Ephesians 1:4 says that God chose everyone in Christ "before the creation of the world to be holy and blameless in his sight." God's desire is not simply to call human beings into life; it is above all to call them into love. Everyone is called to goodness, even before time begins. Not only did God call people to be saints before he created them; he uttered this call before the very world we live in came into being. In this sense ethics comes first. God's call is to be good in the context of a relationship, to be holy and blameless in his sight. However, holiness and spotlessness in his sight can only be adequately measured in terms of love for one's neighbor. As Saint John writes: "If anyone says, 'I love God,' yet hates his brother, he is a liar. For anyone who does not love his brother, whom he has seen, cannot love God, whom he has not seen" (1 John 4: 20). My brother or sister is the one who is naked, hungry, sick, in prison, or lonely, the one who calls me to respond to his or her need. And although I can see external features and characteristics that are common to the other person and to me, there is a secret interiority that I can never pierce, the mysterious core of the person which reflects God's utter incomprehensibility in a singularly unique manner.

Levinas' questioning of our right to be may seem anachronistic in our contemporary world. Should we not simply leave humility behind and focus instead on realizing our true potential? Certain expressions of humility have nightmarish overtones today. In an age that asserts the inviolable nature of human rights, the notion of freely refraining from exercising or defending those rights has a whiff of masochism, if not a decidedly suicidal scent. Why shouldn't I insist on my rights? Why deny myself opportunities for personal enrichment, not to mention the not inconsequential bonus of an enhanced social status? Curtailing rights and curbing freedom are courses of action that grate on us. And yet if we insist on asserting ourselves regardless of others, we will put an unbearable strain on relationships with families and friends; we will even weaken the fabric of politics and society.

Following the seminal 1985 study of Robert Bellah and others in *Habits of the Heart*, Robert Putnam has more recently examined the continuing drift toward individualism in American life. In *Bowling Alone: The Collapse and Revival of American Community*, Putnam argues that the declining social connectedness and civic engagement of Americans since the mid-1960s is potentially harmful to the spiritual, emotional, and physical health of the USA.[3] While Putnam's analysis is devoted to the United States, he hones in on a problem—the decline in community participation—that is common to the entire Western world. Radical individualism corrodes Western culture to an alarming degree. As social psychologist David Myers showed in another recent American study, taking individualism too far ends up ruining individuals.[4]

Individualism and consumerism exert a strong pull on our spirits. We know that money does not lead to happiness, but we still tune in to such programs as *Who Wants to Be a Millionaire.* Even though it has been shown convincingly that, beyond a certain basic level of income, more wealth contributes to declining happiness,[5] our insatiable curiosity about wealthy celebrities suggests either that the statistics are lying, or more plausibly, that we are comatose.

In one sense our world culture has sunk deeply into a coma of the spirit; but there are also small pockets of people who are ascending to an extraordinary goodness. Most of us are probably somewhere in between. We might take the Christian perspective of the seven deadly sins as a way to establish our cultural decay. The seven deadly sins together constitute a perennially valuable yardstick of good and evil. Not that this stopped people from committing these sins in the past, but at least the limits were clearly defined. However, our culture no longer regards these sins as deadly or terminal. Popular magazines and Internet web sites regularly offer questionnaires, tongue-in-cheek, to help us see how entangled in these sins we are. You often get the impression that there is something not quite right with you if you are not relishing at least a couple of the seven capital sins.

Western culture tends to extol capital sins as exhilarating and life-giving. The implication is that you are missing out on life if you are not seriously into pride, greed, gluttony, lust, anger, envy, or sinking into sloth. Our culture encourages us to be *proud* and to pretend that we are more than we really are. Consumerism thrives so much on *greed* that our culture's appetite for having more and more and more threatens to become insatiable. The success and well-being of others fuel resentment—we *envy* what they have and we want it for ourselves. We get so *angry* with people that we lash out without thinking; we feel fury at authorities and institutions and cynically dismiss them or pursue them in court. *Gluttony* has become so entrenched that obesity is reaching epidemic proportions. *Lust*, as always, remains the favorite deadly sin; sex promises such pleasure that it is viewed as a peak secular mystical experience. And all of these sins combine to make us *slothful*, a coma-like state in which our spiritual senses function at an alarmingly low level, and we become unresponsive to the call of goodness.

Our culture may be coma-inducing, but thankfully there are a lot of people who are far from comatose. Even though our cultural environment does not always encourage spiritual aliveness, something in us still celebrates the people who clearly manifest it. There are many people who do not hit the headlines but spend themselves working for the poor. There is the living legacy of Mother Teresa of Calcutta, whose championing of the unwanted and the unloved challenges us to confront our own fear of opening our lives to others. There is the environmental group Greenpeace, whose controversial and headline-grabbing tactics keep environmental issues alive. There are singers like John Lennon whose songs touch our lives in ways we cannot figure and will never forget. There are writers like J.R.R. Tolkien whose magical narratives re-awaken our fatigued spirits. There are Brazilian soccer stars who hone their incredible skills in the slums of Rio and emerge on the world stage to give us welcome glimpses of physical grace and sporting perfection. There are political reconcilers who turn bitterness into hope, like Nelson Mandela, who emerged from his long years in prison full of forgiveness, ready to build a new society in South Africa. There are the little people whose small gestures lead to big changes: like Rosa Parks, of Montgomery, Alabama, who on December 1, 1955, got on a bus and refused to give up her seat at the front to a white man when told to do so.

Such people inspire us. The rest of us would be less without their shining example. Even when these men and women do not speak of God explicitly, they serve his interests all the same. They help to build an era of love and justice. No doubt many of them will be surprised at the Last Judgement when they are rewarded for literally and figuratively feeding the hungry, clothing the naked, visiting the prisoners, and welcoming the refugees. They are inconsistent and imperfect like us all, but in some way their hearts beat in unison with that of their Creator. Something in their spirits partially reflects the brilliant light of God's life.

These people are at the opposite end of the spectrum to the protagonist of the 2002 film *About a Boy*, based upon Nick Hornby's novel of the same name. The film tells the story of a carefree and callow cad who becomes, almost despite himself, a caring and compassionate human being. At the beginning of the film wealthy Londoner Will Freeman, played by Hugh Grant, does not agree with the declaration of the poet John Donne (which he mistakenly attributes to the rock singer Jon Bon Jovi!) that "no man is an island." He is content to play a one-man show and has no intentions of becoming part of an ensemble cast. But through a chance meeting with a twelve-year-old boy called Marcus, he ends up becoming part of a family of sorts. He ceases treating women as objects; he becomes less individualistic and more connected.

The film *About a Boy* raises questions about individualism and suggests that a family structure is necessary, not just in order to flourish but also for the sake of survival.[6] By the end of the film, Will is headed in a healthy direction. Of course there is only so much that a movie can say about such issues. Levinas questions untrammeled freedom and irresponsible egocentricity in a much more radical fashion. We are, he says, called to do more than assume responsibility and recognize the rights of others: we are invited to relegate our own lives to a secondary position. And taking second place demands humility.

In practice, Western culture still favors independence over dependence, action over honest self-knowledge, promotion of the self over the humble service of others. Anything approaching excessive responsibility for others is suspect.[7] But in principle, most of us agree that there is an abiding sense of rightness about taking responsibility for our lives and the lives of others: popular culture repeatedly hammers home this lesson. In the 2003 movie *Bruce Almighty*, Bruce Nolan (Jim Carrey) first encounters God in the form of a black janitor mopping up a warehouse floor, a role played with humor and understated wisdom by Morgan Freeman. Bruce fails to pick up the implicit message about how much God values humble service and identifying with ordinary people. He is given God's job for a while and uses all his divine powers to further his career, giving only an afterthought to his girlfriend, appropriately named Grace (Jennifer Aniston). As the film moves towards a somewhat sentimental conclusion, Bruce learns the supreme importance of caring for others. Rather than working magic tricks as the almighty Bruce, he decides to be the miracle himself by the way he lives as a normal human being. In the 2002 box-office hit *Spider-Man*, the nerdy high school student Peter Parker is told by his Uncle Ben: "With great power comes great responsibility." When Peter suddenly develops arachnid powers, he is faced with the choice of using his newly found gifts for egotistical gain or for the sake of others. Luckily for humanity, the comic book superhero becomes a humble, caring, and socially responsible hero.

In Christianity humility also engenders responsibility, ideally never of a crippling kind. Since everything is understood as gift, the person does what he or she can and entrusts the results to God. There is a bearable lightness about the humble person's responsibility. And there is a deep trust that this responsibility will bear fruit. The trilogy of films based on J.R.R. Tolkien's epic novel *The Lord of the Rings* graphically demonstrates that the power of the ring is too dangerous to be entrusted into the hands of the proud or arrogant, but is instead safest when in the care of humble hobbits.

Although a false humility humiliates and stigmatizes, the genuine virtue elicits admiration. The bestselling French author and philosophy professor André Comte-Sponville suggests that humility is not about ignoring what we are but rather a matter of knowing or recognizing all that we are not.[8] Comte-Sponville declares that it is absurd to want to surpass our status as human beings. Humility is a lucid virtue, the virtue of the human being who knows that he or she is not God. Humility involves the love of truth, and submits itself to truth. To be humble is to love the truth more than oneself. Humility, he writes, is atheism in the first person: the humble person is an atheist when it comes to the first person singular. The humble person does not make himself or herself into God. We can shatter many idols, but perhaps the most difficult one to tear down is the idol that we fashion of ourselves. Humble people know that they are not the center of everything, the axis of the universe. That is part of the honesty of the humble person, a truthfulness free of illusions, including the illusion that would lead to self-glorification. Comte-Sponville distinguishes humility from self-hatred. To hate myself would be to lack the love to which everyone has a right, including myself. Instead of the vocabulary of rights we might think of gratuity. Thus not to love myself would be to deprive myself of that which is beyond every right, but of which we all stand in need. If love were absent, so would humility be, for I would occupy all the available space and there would be no room left for anyone else.

True humility has astonishing force. It is not simply the ability to understand oneself properly, without exaggerating or diminishing one's importance. It is not merely a balanced self-understanding, typified by sober common sense—not that common sense and a balanced self-understanding are not praiseworthy; but humility goes much further. Compared to humility, modesty is a fairly restricted virtue, a virtue of moderation. Genuine humility is much more expansive. Humility is the very life of modesty, its animating principle. Whereas modesty is moderate, humility is either all or nothing. Whereas modesty is characterized by temperance, humility goes all-out. And when it fails to reach its target it does not put the blame on others but admits its own shortcomings. Whereas modesty is more individualistic and more centered on the self, humility is a radical openness toward others. Whereas modesty is concerned with right conduct, humility abandons itself to the perilous adventure of love. In a comatose culture, modesty does not truly wake you up; it just makes you stir in your sleep. Humility of a radical and incisive kind is vital if we are to come to life.

The all or nothing quality of humility is articulated in the call of Peter, James, and John as recounted in the fifth chapter of Luke's Gospel. Jesus invites Peter and his companions to go out onto the lake and cast the nets. Peter is sceptical. Jesus may be the master when it comes to spirituality and carpentry, but Peter knows a lot about the nittygritty of life outdoors and is an expert when it comes to fish. For years he has fished the Lake of Gennesaret. He explains that they have already spent a fruitless night in search of a catch. If the fish have not been there all night, they are not going to surface "miraculously" the next morning. However, out of respect for this well-meaning Rabbi, Peter agrees to cast the nets. Suddenly so many fish are struggling and wriggling that the nets begin to tear. They call on some fishermen in a nearby boat to help haul in the enormous catch. Both vessels almost sink because of the weight of the fish.

Peter the fisherman is fully focused on the task of getting those fish ashore. But as soon as they have reached land, the wonder of this catch begins to dawn upon him. He gets down on his knees before Jesus and says, "Go away from me, Lord; I am a sinful man!" (Luke 5:8) The transcendence of Jesus became visible to Peter in the midst of an everyday activity that he presumed he had mastered— fishing. He had been proud of himself as a talented fisherman. But even in this area of his life, he needs to welcome Jesus as his Savior. Beyond being simply awestruck by the catch, he is now in awe of the holy: he feels how empty he is in the presence of God, how sinful his life is by comparison with the perfection of Jesus' goodness. The experience of the Absolute relativizes everything else. Jesus is the fullness of the divinity, symbolized by the overflowing catch. Peter is the inadequate human being, symbolized by the empty nets the night before meeting the Lord.

Humility begins with Peter's recognition of his own broken humanity. But it does not end there, because Jesus does not depart from this sinful man. It would have been bad news for Peter had Jesus walked away. The good news is that even if Peter feels he has nothing to offer, Jesus can make everything of it. Jesus is an expert at taking nothing and making it more than one could ever dream, ask, or imagine. So he invites Peter to cast his nets out to the deep in a new way, by being a fisherman of human beings. He invites him to unite the humble sense of his own nothingness with the humble recognition of God's greatness. From now on Peter will know that he does not rely on his own power when he casts into the deep world of ministry, but draws from the ever-abundant generosity of God.

Since humility can be interpreted in so many different ways, let me offer a brief description. Like many descriptions, it is a simplification of a term rich in meaning, and inevitably betrays the meaning of what it simplifies. But by highlighting central aspects of humility, it sets the notion into sharper relief and gives a clear point of departure for what I am trying to describe.

Humility includes three essential elements. First, the person must have an awareness of their dependence upon God and others. Second, they must have an awareness of their good and bad sides, their gifts and limitations, their dignity as children of God, and their shortcomings as sinners. And finally, and most importantly, they need to recognize the importance of God and other people through loving and serving them.[9] Since humility is concerned with our relationship to God and others, it is an existential stance that is neither private nor isolating. Rather it expands the horizons of the self to dimensions that exceed it.

We have seen that humility does not enjoy an untarnished reputation. It can be too easily confused with humiliation and servile behavior. Yet when we pay attention to our culture, we realize that humility has somehow "wormed" itself into our consciousness. Not that we are fully aware of it. But we know that arrogance has its limits. We see that, however much we exalt reason and science, they have not solved our problems: we worry that we have become masters of chaos rather than servants of order. We have mixed feelings about our culture-induced coma. Although we know in our heads that certain aspects of our culture are not good for our spirits, we cling to them anyway. It is as though we were saying: "I agree that consumerism is false and superficial, but please don't take away my Gucci shoes!" Our culture is, happily, still breathing, in large part thanks to many secular and religious saints. They are a mixture of good and bad, like most of us, but they are capitalizing on the good. They are humble enough not to want to be everything, but to offer the space of respect to others. They recognize their responsibility in a radical way, casting the nets of their lives into the deep ocean of the world around them. They go in the direction of God and other people; they are pilgrims on the way to a promised land. They are happy to acknowledge how much they owe to God and others; they are realistic about themselves and generous in service.

How did our coma begin? It is time to return to one of the most familiar stories—one that is not at all well understood: the story of our first parents.

2

How the Coma Began

The man and his wife hid from the Lord God.
(Genesis 3:8)

The first parents of humanity were totally awake after God breathed his Spirit into them. Before the Fall, there was no death, simply life in all its fullness, innocence, and love. God gave them a tremendous gift. Their situation was radically different from ours. Even though Christians have been redeemed by Christ, the inclination toward evil is always latent inside, and never goes away fully. But in their case there was no predisposition to evil, no deathly pallor in the soul, no weakness of the will. Yet despite everything they had received, the first couple threw it all away. The serpent's ruse worked and with the sin of our first parents, our comatose state sank in. It is worth looking at the serpent's tactics more closely because we can learn a lot from them. These strategies repeat themselves over and over again throughout history. If we can become more alert to the serpent's cunning and deceit, we might be less likely to fall into a coma ourselves.

Although the story of our first parents uses figurative language, it nevertheless tells us about a decisive deed that

35

occurred at the dawn of human history. The serpent is not literally a serpent. There is almost unanimous agreement among Christians concerning who the serpent stands for: the perennial enemy of humankind, Satan. Regarding the fruit of the tree, there is a more discreet silence.[1] Whatever the fruit, the sin was one of disobedience to God's command, of deliberately going against the Creator's plan by choosing themselves over God. They wanted to be like God, but without God's help and in disaccord with the way God envisaged it. This sin was a rebellion against God and a worshipping of the creature: "They exchanged the truth of God for a lie, and worshiped and served created things rather than the Creator" (Romans 1:25).

There are layers of meaning concealed beneath the dialogue between Eve and the serpent.[2] The dialogue is not as bare as Samuel Beckett's "literature of the unword." Nevertheless it is eloquent in its silences. You have to read between the lines to penetrate the deeper sense of this archetypal story. The serpent implies much in an underhanded way. He begins by sidling up to the woman and posing an apparently innocuous question: "Did God really say, 'do not eat from any tree in the garden?'" The serpent seems to care about what God has to say, but in fact he deliberately misquotes God. He sets God up as a total despot, worse than Attila the Hun. He insinuates that God is nasty, cruel, and even sadistic. The serpent suggests that God set up this wonderful garden of Eden, full of beautiful plants, lush flowers and innumerable trees, and then issued a command saying that Adam and Eve may not taste any of the fruit. But God did not forbid Adam and Eve to eat of any tree in the garden. On the contrary, he gave Adam and Eve almost the free run of the garden. He only stipulated that they were not to eat the fruit of one particular tree. There was free access to every other tree in sight. God forbids Adam and Eve to eat from the fruit of that one tree because he knows that it will harm them. God's command is for their own good. It is given by the One who has granted them the gift of their own lives and the gift of the world as well, more than enough proof of how much he cherishes them.

The serpent is too clever to say something totally untrue. He knows, no pun intended, that Eve would never swallow that. But he realizes that if he mixes a tiny bit of truth with a big lie, he will have much more success. The tiny bit of truth is that God has said that Adam and Eve cannot eat the fruit from a particular tree. But the serpent has taken that little sliver of truth and expanded it to epic proportions—"you must not eat from any tree in the garden." In addition, the serpent slyly intimates that God, the source of all life and goodness, may not be as benign as Eve thinks he is. No wonder the serpent is described as more cunning than any other creature (Genesis 3:1).

If the serpent's strategy is devilishly intelligent, Eve's is plainly foolish. First, and most obviously, she should have called to God for help. She knew in a much more transparent way that we would that God had given her everything. She knew too how near God was, how he walked in the garden in the cool of the day. Given everything that God had done for her, he would have been instantly at her side had she called him, and the serpent for his part would have fled. But Eve was a curious mixture of innocence and arrogance. She was inexperienced when it came to pitting her powers against the wiles of the most cunning creature alive. And she was also excessively confident, precisely because she had never had any reason to worry before. She had lived life with the easy, unguarded confidence of a child. The whole of Eden was at her feet. A curious serpent was nothing to worry about.

Rather than appealing directly to God, as she should have, Eve took it upon herself to act as God's defense attorney. She evidently presumed that on this matter she knew God's mind extremely well. She informed the serpent that God had in fact allowed them to eat of the fruit of the trees in the garden; but as for the fruit of the tree in the center of the garden, God had made it abundantly clear that they should not eat it and *not even touch it on pain of death.* Although Eve was happy with herself for having corrected the serpent on this important question, in fact she made a significant error. Her supposed correction was not a correction at all! Unhappily it demonstrated how little Eve knew God's mind. God never said anything about not touching the fruit of the tree under pain of death. He had only forbidden them from eating it.

Eve actually makes God seem stricter and more demanding than he is. She exaggerates his command. Perhaps she does so because she failed to remember his exact words, or maybe the exaggeration is because she wants to underline the sacredness of God's command because she feels that her allegiance to it is slipping away. In any case the result is that she sees God in a more severe light. She creates her own image of God, a petty and off-putting one at that. She mentions the awful word "death" in connection with God, although all the evidence of her experience shows that God is both the source of life and the one who lovingly keeps her alive.

The serpent picks up on this mention of death, as though he detects a new and darker wavelength in Eve's relationship to God. She now broadcasts on the frequency of fear; she does not speak of a God of love. Ironically, this fear is the result of the serpent's sly question. To double the irony, the serpent now offers a way to allay the fear that he himself has instigated. To triple the irony, the serpent presents himself as her God, as the one who can rescue her from death. He assures her that there is absolutely no chance that she will die as a result of eating the fruit of the tree in the center of the garden.

Lying brazenly, the serpent explains that God wants to keep both her and Adam in slavery. She deludes herself if she imagines she is the queen of Eden. God denies them the pleasure and joy that is rightfully theirs. What is the point of having Eden at their disposal if they miss out on life in all its fullness? The serpent is traditionally identified with Lucifer, meaning "light-bearer," and because this fallen angel, called the "father of lies" by Jesus (John 8:44), still has a glimmer of light left, his lies seem to have the lucidity of truth, interwoven as they are with facts. The serpent's flattering lies have now begun to compromise her innocence. She sees glimpses of a new world that both attracts and repels her. But at that moment she is still free. She can still turn to God. She has only to call him and he will come running. Just as he breathed into Adam and herself at the dawn of creation, now he will breathe new innocence and purity into her, canceling out the serpent's venom.

But she does not want to turn to God. She is hooked. She wants to taste the forbidden fruit. Because she is mistress of Eden—in other words, ruler of the known world—she wants to believe that adding the knowledge of the tree of good and evil to her conquests will have no detrimental effect. She does not want to listen to the voice of impending doom that sounds inside her. She reasons that God's command is superfluous in her case, since she does not need the security of rules and commandments. Nothing has ever gone wrong for her before. Until now everything has been effortless. Everything in creation has gladly bowed before her.

She looks for a clinching argument to justify the course of action she has already chosen. And the serpent is happy to provide it. The serpent now tells Eve the two biggest lies of all: he explains that she will die if she does *not* eat the fruit of that tree. This is a truly preposterous lie because it is the exact opposite of what God said: God told Adam and Eve that they would die if they *ate* the fruit of that tree. If the serpent had told her a lie of this magnitude at the beginning of their dialogue, she would no doubt have turned away. But now that he has steadily weakened her defenses, she is ready to believe this absurdity.

The serpent then declares that not only will eating the fruit of that tree *not* kill her; it will in fact make her much more alive than she is now, radically transforming her. She might be the queen of Eden now, but if she eats of that fruit, she will become the queen of creation, because she will become like God, knowing both good and evil. The serpent, who is far from being God, has now promised divinity to Eve. This is a lie of infinite proportions: you will become like God. The offer seems too good to refuse. And the serpent cannot resist getting in another dig at God, in the form of an additional lie: God fears that she and Adam might eat of the fruit because God knows this will make them like him. He will not be the only God around once Adam and Eve bite into the fruit: he will have serious and implacable rivals on his hands. And Eve is so taken in that she presumes these lies are the helpful advice of a kind-hearted, if unusual, serpent who has gone out of his way to help her. She never stops to think about what could be in it for him.

Her pride is her undoing. She sees sweet fruit that promises pleasure. She believes that she will become godlike when she eats it. She is convinced that God himself is frightened of her. And even though God has given her everything, she does not care about his feelings or his fate at that moment. She sees something for herself, something for her own aggrandizement. She does not think of others. As she stretches out her hand to take the fruit, there is no love in her heart. And in this moment that promises greatest freedom, the queen of Eden becomes a pawn of the serpent in his cruel game of chess. Eve thinks she is attaining new life through eating the fruit, she believes she is about to become a goddess; but in fact she is only sending herself, Adam, and ultimately all of humanity into a long and lifeless coma.

Once they have both eaten the fruit, Adam and Eve realize they are naked. In one sense nothing has changed, since they were naked before. In another sense everything has changed, because now they are ashamed of what was previously good. When they were in a transparent relationship with God, their nakedness, vulnerability and humanity were good things; now that they have severed their relationship with God through disobedience, these same qualities only bring them shame. The real truth behind the twisted lie of the serpent begins to dawn on them: they do indeed know good and evil, but this knowledge does not make them like God at all. In fact, it has the reverse effect, taking away the likeness they had before and making them radically unlike their Creator. Not only does it undo their relationship with

God, it also undermines their love for each other. They cannot bring themselves to be honest or open with one another. Instead, they hide the humiliation of who they are under the cover of fig leaves.

When they hear the sound of God taking his morning walk in the garden, Adam and Eve hide from him. Previously they rejoiced when they heard his footsteps; now they flee. God has not changed—they have. Now they can no longer be themselves before God. They are no longer loving and innocent, they have become repellent to themselves, and they are afraid to bring this guilt and misery into God's presence. They are unable to utter the simple words, "sorry, please forgive us." Sadly they no longer seem to believe in God's love. If God were to leave them to their own devices, that would be the end of the relationship. Luckily for them, God reaches out to save the relationship before it disintegrates completely. God calls out to Adam, "Where are you?" It is a big question: not only is he asking Adam where he is in the garden, he also asks him where he is in his life and spirit. God throws them a life buoy before they fully sink into the mire of their own making. God opens a window of opportunity for them, delicately inviting Adam to be humble, and to own up to his guilt. But Adam has now been infected by the poisonous deceit of the serpent. He cannot bring himself to be fully truthful or transparent.

So rather than telling God where he is, Adam says that he was afraid when he heard God in the garden since he knew he was naked, and so he made sure to hide himself. God, however, does not give up on Adam. He gives him another graced opportunity, inviting him to explain how he came to discover he was naked. Again Adam refuses to take responsibility: this time he blames Eve, in an effort to move the spotlight from himself. He tells God that it was Eve who gave him the fruit which he ate. And in a pointed addition, he remarks that it was God himself who gave Eve to Adam. The implication is that none of this would have happened if God had been smart enough not to create Eve as Adam's companion in the first place. Not only has Adam put the blame on Eve, he has also subtly pointed the finger at God himself. God turns to Eve to offer her a chance to be humble and truthful. But she cannot rise to the occasion either. Taking her cue from Adam she decides to blame someone else too, in her case the serpent.

The evasive and irresponsible replies of Adam and Eve are truly sad. God offered them the chance to end their lies and pretense, to own up to their disobedience. But they never said the simple words, "sorry, please forgive us." It is such a pity that Adam and Eve do not trust God enough to bring this shame and guilt before him. He is still the loving God who gave them so much. But each time God offers them a step forward they take two steps back.

It is after the Fall that prayer begins. Prayer does precisely what Adam and Eve failed to do when God called them in the garden: they failed to raise their minds and hearts to him. They not only covered their bodies before God; they also hid their hearts from him. Biblically, the heart has always been regarded as the true center of the person, the place where relationships are won or lost, the place where either life or death is chosen. But as Scripture tells us, there is nothing more devious than the heart (Jeremiah 17:9). If we are to cope with the comatose culture we live in, we need to raise our minds and hearts above it. We need to focus our attention on whatever is noble, lofty, and pure. We need to give time to God.

Adam and Eve wanted their kingdom to come and their will to be done. They wanted to run the show and to make themselves the privileged center of reality. The words of Jesus invite us to place his kingdom, not ours, at the center. He suggests that we store up our treasure in heaven so that our hearts may be there as well. We need not worry about not having enough. We will always have what we need. We do not know how much future we have before us. The birds in the sky do not sow or cultivate or gather into barns, yet they do not starve because the heavenly Father feeds them. And we human beings, who are made in God's image, are worth so much more than they are. So Jesus invites us to seek the things that make this image of God shine within us—humility, goodness, righteousness, purity, faith, love, friendship with God. And he assures us that all of the rest will be given to us as well without us even having to ask. We will have the infinite richness of God's presence in this world and paradise in the next.

Prayer is neither primarily about me nor the expansion of my personal empire. It is fundamentally directed towards others. In line with his stress upon the importance of the other, Levinas insists that prayer should never be for oneself, but always for the other.[3] This is an invaluable principle as long as it does not become an absolute one; indeed Levinas himself is willing to temper it in certain circumstances. For example, one can pray for oneself when this self is the larger "self" of Israel that is being ridiculed or oppressed: "This is not in the name of any nationalist egoism. The people of Israel, we must remember, are the bearers of revelation."[4] Second, he says that if I am suffering, I can apply prayer to this painful situation on the condition that I am praying for God's suffering in me, since God always suffers in every human suffering.

Although these exceptions might seem to be the result of the application of hair-splitting casuistry, I believe that they reflect a profound wisdom. First of all, no one can believe alone and no one can pray alone. We are always part of a community. Second, God does not leave us isolated and forlorn in our suffering, but carries our burden with us. Of course it is not easy to believe that God could be so much on our side as to suffer with us. In his searing story of his time in Auschwitz, *Night*, Elie Wiesel recounts a haunting episode that shows how suffering tempts us with atheism. An angel-faced boy is one of three victims hanging from the gallows, and dies a slow and agonizing death. A bystander asks: "'Where is God now?' And I heard a voice within me answer him: 'Where is He? Here He is—He is hanging here on this gallows.'" Does Wiesel mean by this that his child-hood image of God is dying, and that now he is beginning to see how God suffers in and with us; or is he saying that God and meaning are dying for him at that moment as the little boy swings from the gallows? In fact it is the latter. Ever since, Wiesel has been wrestling with faith, refusing an unthinking atheism, yet finding it hard to believe in a God who continues to perplex him.

In any case, Levinas gives us a salutary reminder that prayer is not a self-centered act but an act whose center is outside of us. This is a helpful wake-up call. If we forget the other and wallow in an ocean of emotions, this is not prayer. Prayer does not enfold us in a comfortable cocoon; it opens us up to the world. Eternal rest is for later. Now is the time of vigilance, of watchfulness and wakefulness. But our spiritual yearnings can often cloak an unhealthy narcissism. We look for wholeness, we seek meaning, we want to find our real selves and center in a fragmented world. But this is merely thinking of what we lack, of what we need.

In prayer we turn our hearts to a mysterious and loving God with sighs and feelings that even we cannot comprehend, that only the Holy Spirit can truly articulate. Theology needs to be linked to this primordial experience. Theology takes the form of conjectures, assumptions, clarifications, definitions, and explanations. These all have their place. But beneath them all and prior to them all is an overriding experience of grace and worship. If theology loses this vital connection, its shimmer and sparkle inevitably dim. It is certainly difficult to see more than a faint gleam of a relationship which is so bright at its core that it remains stubbornly opaque. Nevertheless, something of this glowing mystery should filter through into theological discourse.

The language of prayer is a language suffused with reverence for God. It is the language of the real self. The real self is not the possessive, grasping ego, intent on reducing everything to an object as it strives to satisfy its own needs. I only find my true self through responding to the call of God, the "where are you?" that he addressed to Adam in the Garden of Eden. But since we no longer live in paradise, God cannot be seen, he can only be heard. And we need to be careful when we talk about God in an academic way because we can easily make graven images of him. Our concepts can never explain the utter mystery of God, and can never reduce him to horizons where we are sovereign.

In Christian faith, prayer is to the soul what oxygen is to the body. Without it our spirits shrivel up and die. But because prayer is above all an act of love, we also should beware of idolizing prayer itself. Although we should devote time to prayer each day, we should not absolutize the act of praying. Only God is absolute. Prayer is one way, albeit crucial, of raising our minds and hearts to God. But we can also raise our minds and hearts to God through serving others. And thus, at certain times, we may be invited to sacrifice prayer in order to help others. This is evident in the journey the Virgin Mary makes to help her cousin Elizabeth during her pregnancy. It would have been natural for Mary to stay at home rather than rush to her cousin's assistance. After all, she herself had more than enough to worry about: she was shortly to give birth to the Redeemer of the world. It would have been perfectly understandable had she remained in Nazareth and taken the greatest care of this divine child. Why run the risk of exposing this tiny unborn life to danger by rushing off to her cousin's side? But it is precisely because God is already in her heart, and not only in her womb, that she is generous. She trusts that he is there to help her and to bless her efforts. She knows that he will provide for those who humbly trust in him. God will take care of her pregnancy, more especially because she is taking care of Elizabeth's pregnancy.

Mary had to travel a long distance in order to be at the side of Elizabeth. The wonder of prayer is that we can immediately place ourselves in the presence of God. There is no need to make an appointment weeks or even days in advance. God is willing to meet us in the here and now. God is so easily accessible because he is attentive to us in a loving way every moment of our lives. He knows what we need. Sometimes we treat God as especially dull-witted and slow, since we spend so much of our prayer reminding him of what we want. If even the hairs on our head are counted, if even a sparrow does not fall to the ground without God's knowledge, it is preposterous to presume that he does not notice our needs. He is after all a Father who takes a hugely personal interest in each one of us. However, this is not to deny that we are actively encouraged to ask God for all we need. But we are to ask in a simple and trusting way. We can be assured that he will not give us stones when we ask for bread, or snakes when we look for fish.

Because we receive time piece by piece, moment by moment, we know that something is right for us today, but cannot tell whether it will be beneficial for us tomorrow. So we must trust that God, who possesses time completely, acts in our best interests when he does not answer our prayer in the present. The day will come when we will feel deep gratitude to him for denying us in the past. God may be giving us something marvellous in the long term by apparently not answering our prayers now.

Jesus offers us the archetype of every prayer. It begins with the words, "Our Father." The first word is already a demonstration that we never pray alone as isolated selves, but always as part of a community. The second word encapsulates a quantum leap from the mechanical understanding of God as a remote master to be feared above all else. It also reflects a truly intimate and privileged relationship. What is even more extraordinary is that since Jesus asks us to use the word "Father," his Father must enjoy us addressing him as such. It is not as if he reluctantly admits us to this relationship. God never does things by halves. The next phrase, asking that God's name be hallowed, reminds us that both awe and intimacy have their place before our Father. When we speak of the Father, we are using a word, but it is like an arrow leaving a bow that never reaches its target, for God's utter holiness and goodness always remain essentially beyond our range. The challenge is to hold together profound reverence for God and the deep intimacy of being his sons and daughters.

We ask that God's kingdom may illuminate our world, that the darkness of a culture of death will give way to an enlightened culture of life. We ask that we be given the grace to surrender our lives to God's loving plan, which is nothing other than that everyone should be good. We humbly ask God for our daily needs. We ask forgiveness for all that we have received but not reciprocated. We are in debt not only to God but to everyone from our families to our friends, from our neighbors to our nations. To varying degrees we have received love, education, employment, security, recognition, and success. We promise to forgive the small number of people who are indebted to us materially or morally. And finally, knowing how little we are, we humbly pray that God will keep us close to him and safe from temptations. We pray with the transparency and humility of trusting children, knowing that our God is an incredible mixture of compassion and strength. He knows our weaknesses yet he is above them and so he can raise us up, for to him belong the kingdom and the power and the glory.

Towards the end of the Our Father, we ask to be kept safe from temptations. I want to begin the next chapter discussing *The Matrix*, a film whose religious themes have "led" many people to talk about faith in endless website discussions. Like many other offerings in our popular culture, this film implicitly promises to wake us up. This much heralded cult film and its two sequels were major box-office hits around the world. Partly because it is an amazing smorgasbord of philosophical, religious and cultural influences, everyone can find something in *The Matrix* to fit with their world-view. But does the film harmonize with the forgiving love of Jesus? And if it does not, can *The Matrix* deliver on its big promise: to rouse us from our stupor?

3

False Hope

You take the blue pill and the story ends. You wake in your bed and believe whatever you want to believe. You take the red pill and you stay in Wonderland and I show you how deep the rabbit-hole goes. Remember, all I'm offering is the truth, nothing more.

The Matrix

Sometimes people have the false hope that a loved one will emerge instantly from a coma, open their eyes, give everyone a big smile and promptly get up from their hospital bed. But waking up from a coma is generally a more gradual process. Each case is different, but often patients open their eyes, seem to be awake, then fall back into the coma. As they become conscious for longer periods, they begin to move their arms and legs at random. Then they utter sounds. They steadily gain control of their bodily movements and speech, moving their limbs in directions they choose and saying meaningful things when they open their mouths. Yet even after they are discharged from the hospital they may have problems with remembering things, with concentrating on what they are doing, and even with such basic things as having enough energy to cope with a full waking day.

Even though miraculous improvements in comas sometimes occur, there can be unrealistic hopes about emerging from this condition, just as there can be exaggerated expectations about emerging from spiritual sleepiness as well. I want to juxtapose false hopes of emerging from the spiritual coma of Western culture with the true way of vulnerable love modeled by Jesus.

Two thousand three saw the release of the two eagerly-awaited sequels to *The Matrix*: *The Matrix Reloaded* and *The Matrix Revolutions*. They both had even more spectacular special effects and more elaborate martial arts than the original film; in fact the story line of the second and third films lost out to the special effects. And amidst all the frenetic action there was even more violence. Yet the first film of the series has found cult status because it has more to offer than stylized conflict.

The Matrix was thoroughly entertaining and a resounding box-office success as well. Beneath the surface enjoyment, *The Matrix* is so pregnant with religious and cultural references that many movie buffs have discerned deeper meanings within it. Whether you are into Alice in Wonderland, Plato, Buddha, or Jesus, this film resonates with at least some of your convictions and beliefs. In fact for many devoted fans, seeing the movie was such a deeply spiritual experience that they went to see it again . . . and again.

What I want to look at here is not the religious subtext, but its attitude to violence. Violence has become the stereotypical response of action movies to cultural scenarios that induce comas of one kind or another, whether these comas be lives of quiet desperation or bland conformity. Despite the style and beauty of the film, I wonder whether at heart it isn't yet another glorification of brute force.

The protagonist of the cult 1999 film *The Matrix* is Thomas Anderson (played by Keanu Reeves), a compliant software employee by day and a crack computer hacker called Neo by night. He feels that there is something more to the world around him than he sees. He meets the beautiful Trinity, a fellow hacker who has joined an underground resistance group that has awakened to the fact that the world as we perceive it does not exist. The world human beings take to be real is simply a virtual reality computer program. This "matrix" generates the illusion of real life in order to keep human beings in a zone of comfort, while their electrical energy is siphoned off by the artificial intelligence which effectively runs the world. Trinity introduces Neo to Morpheus, the leader of the rebels.

Morpheus confronts Neo with a crucial choice. He can either return to his anesthetized existence or he can truly live. If Neo takes the blue pill, he will return happily to the simulated world he has been living in all his life; if he takes the red pill, he will see the world as it really is. The blue and red pills could be taken for metaphors of the alternatives Levinas presents us with: totality or infinity.

Levinas' blue pill is the world in which we find ourselves. At its basis is a *philosophical* computer program, if you like, a way of looking at the world where we abstract from the particular characteristics of things and put them under an overarching totality. So we say that Mark and David are the same because they are human beings, my Arabian horse and my neighbor's red-footed tortoise are both part of the animal kingdom, and so on. The whole realm of being seen this way is a realm of sameness. We do not cherish the uniqueness and particularity of people. We do not respect their otherness. Instead we grasp them under a reductive concept. It is like the woman who saw a familiar-looking face before her at the train station. She grabbed the man by the elbow and said, "Oh Greg, you've changed so much! You used to be muscular and now you look positively emaciated. You used to have blond hair but now it is black. You used to be tall and now you're—." The man, who all this time had been trying unsuccessfully to get a word in, suddenly lost his patience and exclaimed, "Wait a minute, I'm not Greg, I'm Stephen!" The woman's jaw dropped, but then she recovered her composure somewhat, leaned towards him and, in a loud conspiratorial whisper, exclaimed, "Don't tell me you've changed your name as well!"

As well as depriving others of their transcendence, Levinas believes we have also seriously compromised our moral sense. This is not to suggest that he has any intention of lamenting the disappearance of the good old days. After all, there was nothing endearing about the barbarism that sullied the twentieth century. But he does believe that the whole moral enterprise has today become dubious, if not derisory.[1] In terms of *The Matrix*, why bother going for the red pill? The reason for this unhappy situation is that over and over again in the course of the twentieth century, people abandoned the supposedly eternal laws of morality, replacing them with makeshift and immoral rules. This becomes obvious when we reflect on how the fact of war has compromised morality. When nations go to war, they replace the sacrosanct laws of morality with opportunistic principles. When we are at war, a country we previously regarded as benign or as at least harmless is suddenly transformed into something demonic. This metamorphosis is evident at the level of language. Enemy troops are labeled as fanatics whereas ours are extolled as brave. If the deliberate killing of their innocent civilians is deemed necessary, we decide that it only amounts to collateral damage. The war itself is often called an operation of some sort, as though it were a surgical removal of unhealthy tissue carried out by someone who had taken the Hippocratic Oath, and so on. And in case our consciences begin to bother us, we only have to pick up a newspaper or tune into television in order to have our minds laid to rest by politicians and media gurus who tell us that although morality is alright in principle, it is simply too naïve when it comes to the bloody business of armed conflict:

> In peace there's nothing so becomes a man
> As modest stillness and humility:
> But when the blast of war blows in our ears,
> Then imitate the action of the tiger;
> Stiffen the sinews, summon up the blood.
> Disguise fair nature with hard-favour'd rage.
> (Shakespeare, *Henry V*, Act 3, Scene 1)

Levinas disagrees. If we accept the suspension of *eternal* moral principles for the sake of war, how can we claim that they are once again binding when we return to a situation of peace? How can we blithely return legitimacy to something we have implicitly declared to be illegitimate when it suited us? War, by holding morality in abeyance for its duration, also abolishes its credibility in peacetime. If we are encouraged to hate our enemies in war, to lie to them, to use dirty tactics to prevail over them, it will be more than tempting to be dishonest, cold, and underhanded at other times as well. It is easier to flaunt the demands of "ordinary" morality when gruesome wartime deeds have increased your threshold of tolerance for minor misdemeanors. What's the big deal about telling a lie in everyday life when you have incessantly resorted to misleading propaganda in war? If we allow morality to slip away during war, we will not be able to maintain it in peacetime.

But Levinas' focus is wider than military actions: he goes beyond the meaning of war in the literal sense. When he talks about war, he is not thinking primarily of armed conflict between groups or nations. Levinas discerns something warlike and proud in the way we *are*. To be is to exercise power, to assert oneself, to struggle for recognition. By the mere fact of existing, each of us displays an inherent aggression, however unintentional it may be. To live is to hold and exert power. There are certainly various economic, environmental, and other theories to account for why we possess and exercise power, but fundamentally Levinas links it to the fact that reality is simply that way. In this context we find one of Pascal's thoughts among the series of epigraphs at the beginning of Levinas' *Otherwise than Being or Beyond Essence*, ". . . That is my place in the sun. This is how the usurpation of the whole world began."

Actual war maims and kills people. But the gung-ho way we behave in civilian life is also damaging. Although there is no blood spilt in most everyday conflicts, there is still a lot of damage done. We can see warlike situations everywhere from the stampedes of January sales, to the harried driver who lowers the window of his (or increasingly her) stylish red sports car and yells abuse or gives you the finger.² Trite as it may sound, basic good manners are a modest way of resisting war. Now I am not claiming that politeness is the solution to war. We know that polite people are not always as virtuous as they seem; polished manners can hide a lot of shady things. The knight in shining armor whose chivalrous prose woos a young woman on an internet dating site might not be the tall, good-looking, single young hunk he pretends—he could be a 51-year-old hypocrite, feigning what he does not feel, with a wife and children at home.

But that is not to say that good manners are worthless. In fact, as we know, common courtesy can make an uncommon difference in our lives. And even if I am not quite the self-forgetful and kind person that my manners imply, at least if I am trying to be that kind of person, good manners can help me in the quest. They might not express the full truth about me now. But that need not render refined manners untrue. They can also convey the truth of the person I am actively seeking to become. I can use the language and gestures of gallantry to manifest my desire to be considerate to everyone, thoughtful and obliging, attentive and kind. Although I know that I am far from such active benevolence, by anticipating this state through good manners, I am already helping myself attain it.

Is this a lack of authenticity, a failure to be myself? It is if I am an utterly callous cad just trying to hoodwink you into believing I am Mr. Right in order to get kicks out of your misery, or to exploit your good faith. But if I practice good manners as an integral part of my efforts to be a truly good person, that is something altogether different. However mannerly we are on the surface, we know that inside parts of us can be rude and overbearing, jealous and resentful, character traits of which we are not proud. To become our true selves we need to cast a lot of this dross aside.

So we are not contributing to the well-being of humanity by venting our spleen, even if it is in the interests of authenticity. I do not think it would be a good idea for me to hurl epithets in your direction, even if your actions served to cast doubts on your parentage! Not only would this expression of anger on my part make me an even more bitter person; it would also make it difficult for you to draw out your best self when we are together. In fact you might well be tempted to draw out an Uzi submachine gun. But if I am courteous I can coax goodness out of you. By doing something as basic as embracing the laws of etiquette, I can encourage both of us toward moral excellence.

In Levinas' opinion, our culture is asleep. Waking up is about respecting other people as truly other; it is about refusing the temptation to reduce them to objects.[3] *The Matrix* also believes that Western culture has put people's spirits to sleep. Yet despite its kinetic energy and visual style, it does not succeed in overturning this aggressive and competitive world. When Neo is disconnected from the plugs that have fed him a virtual reality and undergoes a baptismal kind of experience, this graphic symbolism of death to the old self seems to promise what it signifies. But in fact the opposite occurs: his ego reaches even more imperial proportions. The only self-emptying that occurs in the wake of his rebirth is when Neo vomits a viscous white liquid on the floor of the rebel spaceship! There are token external signs of change, such as a more ascetic diet and lifestyle. But in fact the encounter with Morpheus leads to increased power, to an expansion of the ego's territory. Neo discovers that excellence in any skill, whether it is martial arts or flying a helicopter, can be downloaded into one's brain in seconds. When he sets out to rescue Morpheus from the hands of the agents of the matrix, Neo asks for a lot of guns. So a film that promised a quantum leap in the understanding of reality ends up with an old-fashioned violent shootout. Despite the occasional nod in the direction of humility, Neo takes the road to power. Even though the name Neo means new, there is something old and clichéd about finding the way to enlightenment through automatic weapons fire.

The brilliantly staged gun battles, the mesmerizing images of bullets ripping through columns of sheer concrete, the computer-enhanced stunts, all serve to camouflage the lack of any decisive transformation in the world. When Trinity and Neo fire endless rounds of ammunition in two-handed gunfights with scores of bad guys, the cameras adoringly relishing it all in super slow motion. You wonder whether human beings have really evolved to a higher level, or whether these slick scenes unintentionally condone the mayhem of American high school massacres.

The Matrix is a graphic example of a widespread tendency in our culture: the mistaken belief that we can solve our problems through a show of strength and aggressive action. The truth is that if we rely on our own powers to escape from our comatose state, we will only become more embedded within it. We need something, or more correctly, Someone beyond ourselves. How then is it possible to transcend this totalitizing matrix that reduces others to sameness, that forces us to play roles that are not our own? Through grace, which helps us find a new way of relating to each other and to the world around us.[4] It is a way of relating to people that does not reduce them into ciphers or concepts. It is a way of being open to the world that does not try to pin everything down and petrify it. George Steiner makes a stunning use of the image of the Annunciation in conveying transformative experience: something grave and beautiful invades "the small house of our cautionary being. If we have heard rightly the wing-beat and provocation of that visit, the house is no longer habitable in quite the same way as it was before."[5]

What is grace? It is the experience of God's love turning toward us, inviting us to new life, showing our resistances and yet offering to heal them by bringing us into communion with himself. Grace is prophetic and provocative, it is something unimaginable and undefined. It sweeps over us from beyond any horizon which we control. It comes from beyond the closed circle of the world and so it cannot be integrated into this world. When we are really asleep, grace comes as a short sharp shock, as in Yahweh's question to Cain: "Where is your brother Abel?" (Genesis 4:9). And sometimes we respond brazenly, as Cain did, "Am I my brother's keeper?" It is telling that Cain's response takes the form of a question, for he cannot bring himself to make an outright denial. Inside he knows that he is responsible for Abel's murder. Here we see that grace, when it needs to be, can be rudely intrusive, for Cain never asked to be Abel's brother in the first place. Neither do we ask to be brothers or sisters of other human beings. We simply are.

At the core of our being there is a desire for God of which Saint Augustine speaks so eloquently. It is a curious desire because the more we nourish it, the more intense it becomes; the human spirit truly longs for God since he is more intimate to us than we are to ourselves. The great

Swiss Protestant theologian Karl Barth speaks of the event of revelation as rupturing the world, grasping and then mastering the person. According to the German Jesuit theologian Karl Rahner, the human being exists at once in nature and beyond nature, called continually and inescapably into communion with Christ, whether he or she accepts this call or not.

There is a summons in Levinas too, although it seems more of a moral imperative than a loving invitation. Does this sterner perspective reflect an austere image of the Old Testament God? I think it is more due to the fact that Levinas finds the word "love" to be weighed down by too many ambiguities. In his later writings and interviews he did endorse a "severe" form of love, purged of egoism and self-interest. Perhaps too Levinas' emphasis on the commanding nature of the ethical call was influenced by his own exposure to misery and suffering. He spent the war doing forced labor in a German camp for military prisoners, while his parents and brothers were executed by the Nazis. Afterwards Levinas was angry with God because he felt he was absent at Auschwitz. And he stubbornly decided that even if God were to be unfaithful, he would remain faithful—an inversion of 2 Timothy 2:13 ("if we are faithless, he will remain faithful").

Whether we are Jewish or not, we should not let our thinking forget the sinister shadow of Auschwitz that lurks behind us. Auschwitz is above all an actual place where unspeakable things happened, a harrowing symbol of the extermination of millions of Jews throughout the Nazi era. It has come to represent all the horrific world events that have fractured sense and meaning. Auschwitz is not dead: this horrible memory still threatens to put our world into a coma from which it might never wake up. There is also a darkness looming over our culture because of the many other inhuman acts that have cast a pall over the last century. Yet the long and terrible wound of Auschwitz can keep us vigilant and awake, precisely because it has sliced open the flaccidity of complacent theology and self-indulgent spirituality. With the memory of Auschwitz in our hearts, we more easily resist the temptation to descend into sweet and saccharine spirituality, or to become warm and fuzzy Christians. It ensures that we will remain real, even if reality is not always as nice as we would like it to be.

Auschwitz raised troubling questions for the Jewish people. Many Jews had taken God's omnipotence for granted because of the stories of creation and Exodus. But this understanding of God abruptly went up in smoke, like the clouds that rose from the chimneys of the death camps. How could they reconcile the Creator of the universe and the Mighty Liberator of the Israelites with the apparent powerlessness of this "Omnipotent" One in the face of Jewish suffering during the Holocaust? After wrestling with this agonizing question for a long time, Levinas came up with a novel answer. He decided that God had pulled back as it were, not because he did not care, but in order to allow the rest of us freely to decide what kind of people we wanted to be: lifesavers or killers. God withdraws in self-effacement in order to allow human beings the space and freedom either to respond to others or else to petrify into stony egoism.

God does not so much withdraw as empty himself in the life of Jesus. The life of Jesus is both an all-consuming response of love to the Father and a complete surrender of himself to us. When we contemplate the life and death of

Jesus we begin to realize that his omnipotence is nothing like the omnipotence of the guns that are adoringly photographed in *The Matrix*. (To be fair, there is a moment of insight at the end of the movie when Neo realizes that the bullets he always presumed to be live ammunition are in fact only blank charges when it comes to the higher life of the spirit). Jesus' omnipotence is not an infinitely arithmetical extension of human power. It is not the limitless ability to wipe out all the bad guys, which is a harmful fantasy, the kind of wishful and unrealistic thinking that characterizes false hope. Instead it is omnipotence of an entirely different order, one that we ourselves could not dream of. It is the omnipotence of love that goes beyond all frontiers. Unlike Neo, Jesus does not exercise his power in order to halt the bullets that are fired at him. Neither does he use his power to eliminate the villains who target him. Rather his omnipotence manifests itself in the love with which he allows himself to be wounded and killed. It is the astonishing power of a love that suffers on behalf of everyone who is bad so that we can become good. The love of Jesus invites us to re-think omnipotence: any fool can start a war, plant a bomb or shoot innocent people in order to make a name for himself. But only God has the absolute power of compassion that enables him to empty himself to the extent of dying on a cross and forgiving his murderers at the same time. The example of Jesus teaches us that omnipotence without love is not divine but all too human.

The humility of the infinite mystery that is God also finds expression in the Old Testament. Take, for instance, those breathtaking verses from 1 Kings 19:11-12: "Then a great and powerful wind tore the mountains apart and shattered the rocks before the Lord, but the Lord was not in the wind. After the wind there was an earthquake, but the Lord was not in the earthquake. After the earthquake came a fire, but the Lord was not in the fire. And after the fire came a gentle whisper." The soft and non-intrusive voice heard by Elijah is fascinating because it speaks of a humility that is not of this world. And precisely because humility is so otherworldly, it disturbs and upsets our mundane categories, our habitual mind-sets. The voice that presents itself to Elijah in such a vulnerable way is a voice that has no home within our coherent and common-sense conception of reality. This voice never takes up an abode in our world. It is like an object from outer space that penetrates the atmosphere but vanishes with only a trace before it can touch the earth.

The hardly perceptible effect of the voice in our world is the humble nearness of God. Paradoxically, God manifests his greatness by not exercising the fullness of his power. He does not force our obedience. Yet inside our hearts there is something infinite that links us to God: this something is the world of desires. For our wishes, dreams, and desires are the only infinite things about us. Our deepest desires project us beyond the world of our own needs, and urge us to service.

The desire to go beyond ourselves is within us even at those moments when we experience contentment and plenitude in our lives. Spiritual disaffection often coincides with material fullness: it is mostly the richest people who feel spiritually most empty. Even at the best of times, there is always a desire within us to go beyond a happiness that is solely for ourselves, and instead to live a life of selfless service to the other. This desire is the humble presence of God, the gentle breeze hardly noticed by Elijah. It is seen in the serene stillness of silent lakes, it swooshes in a sheet of sudden rain, it bleeds in the red glow of the setting sun, it dances on the laughing lips of little ones, and is chiselled deep into the furrowed faces of grizzled fishermen. But most of all it pleads and whispers inside our own hearts. It is an offer that we are free to decline. Yet it always abides. This desire is the one fundamental love that breathes inside our souls, the love of God. Therefore life is not about the search for all the small loves, but instead finds its flowering in the joy of being found by Love itself.

This desire to go beyond ourselves is graphically illustrated in Levinas' juxtaposition of the journey of Abraham and that of Ulysses. Abraham left a familiar and known land in order to travel towards that which was distant and foreign. He left his own land and culture, never to return, and journeyed to somewhere totally unknown. Compared with Abraham's pilgrimage, the voyage of Ulysses was circular, starting from Ithaca and returning there. Levinas sees Ulysses' journey as paradigmatic of the trajectory of Western philosophy, which never truly encounters otherness, and ultimately never relinquishes the comforts of domesticity. Despite his lengthy explorations, Ulysses returned to the place where he started. Ulysses' journey was also questionable from a moral point of view: in the opening lines of Homer's great epic, the hero of the Odyssey is described as *polutropos*, "a man of many turns or wiles," and was later consigned to hell by no less than Dante because of his insatiable quest to plumb the depths of wickedness as well as ascend the heights of virtue.

By following the desire for God implanted within our spirits, we can find a way out of the coma. Now it is time to look at some criteria of spiritual aliveness so that we can recognize and embrace this wakeful state in our own lives.

4

Signs of Wakefulness

Sleepers Awake!

J.S. Bach, *Cantata Number 140*

Religion in general is in the business of waking people up. We have examined a false way of rousing people from sleep, one that encourages us to assert ourselves without regard for the welfare of others, in an implicitly or explicitly violent manner. Now it is time to point to what being awake means concretely in our lives.

Wakefulness is about being aware. When you are awake you are aware of things. You live in the present moment. There are many delightful stories from the Buddhist tradition about awareness. One of the most "Buddhist" descriptions of living in the now is Jesus' invitation in Matthew 6: 25-34 not to worry about tomorrow nor about food and clothing. In fact, "invitation" is too weak a word: Jesus *commands* his listeners not to worry. Yet this is not a burdensome command since Jesus gives persuasive reasons why worry does not make sense. First of all, when we look at the birds of the air, we can see how our heavenly Father feeds them. It does not take the genius of an Einstein to understand that we are much more valuable in

God's eyes than they are. Watching low-flying swifts skimming the tiled terra cotta roofs of Rome in summer, I cannot help thinking of this appeal of Jesus. Swifts do not gather into barns; they do not even have beaks to stick out and grab their prey. These sleek sooty-brown birds are experts at flying: they make lightning-fast turns and sudden swoops, opening their mouths wide enough to scoop up flying insects. Swifts are so aerodynamically advanced that they put the most sophisticated and expensive fighter jets to shame. They are fed by the heavenly Father. When autumn is approaching, they do not think of accumulating reserves. They migrate in large flocks with their joyful screeches, trusting that there will always be flies, moths, and other flying insects to feed on. They know that they will arrive at a warm place. And when spring comes round again, they will be back, eating, drinking, and even taking mini-naps on the wing.

But most important of all, worrying about our lives is an insult to God, however unintentional this offense may be. By worrying we implicitly doubt God's goodness and power. Not only is the Father caring enough to discern our needs; he is also powerful enough to satisfy them. It ultimately comes down to trust: are we willing to trust God enough to focus our lives on his agenda, all the while confident that he will take care of our everyday worries?

The simple insights of Brother Lawrence of the Resurrection (1614-1691), a humble French Carmelite brother who spent thirty years working in the community kitchen, offer an interesting angle on awareness. Brother Lawrence realized in his heart that God was present to the world he created and specifically to him. God's presence generally escapes our awareness. Sure, we are often aware of the world around us, but we tend to forget that the one who created this world did not just down tools, shut up shop and go away once the world was made. In fact God stayed on. He is "the still point of the turning world" as the poet T.S. Eliot put it in "Burnt Norton." He is present to each of us. Brother Lawrence made a habit of constantly talking to God. What did he talk about? Simple things for the most part. But to help give him subject matter for these conversations, Lawrence also made an effort to imagine all the positive things about God—his love, his mercy, his kindness, and so on. And by virtue of this simple method, Brother Lawrence succeeded in spending every moment of his life in God's presence. In other words, he lived in the truth of an awareness that the vast majority of us never even wake up to. He thus raised awareness to new heights, by going beyond mere appearances to the hidden presence of God that is always there if only we have eyes to see. The practice of the presence of God is awareness at its utter fullness, because it is awareness of that which, although invisible, is also most real.

Wakefulness is about searching. To be a searcher is to be humble. Take the Magi, the model seekers of Jesus. They were not curiosity seekers. It was the truth that guided their quest. Matthew's Gospel explains that their search originated when they noticed an unusual star in the east They were astrologers, a highly respected profession in the ancient world. "Where is the one who has been born king of the Jews? We saw his star in the east and have come to worship him" (Matthew 2:2). You can tell by the way they talk that they were anything but hucksters who gave dubious and vague advice on horoscopes: you know the sort of thing—"you are about to find new romance in your life."

Tradition tells us that there were three wise men. Did they live in the same town or village? Or were they from different places? We do not know. I like to believe that they were from different countries, and that each of them independently noticed the star, took out charts and diagrams, pored over these maps of the heavens night and day, trying to discover the meaning of this exceptional sight that lit up the night sky. They must have been humble men, marveling at the vastness of God's creation, the enormity of the heavens, and the beauty of the stars that were scattered across the sky like jewels. They must have been honest men, anxious to understand the truth itself rather than to fabricate a truth in their own image. And their honesty as well as their knowledge revealed to them that this star was a sign from God, the herald of the birth of the King of the Jews.

They set out, and somewhere along the journey, their three paths converged. None of them knew how long this journey would be, none of them was sure if their provisions would last, all of them were ignorant of the territories that lay ahead. Would they encounter hostile tribes? Would there be high mountains and immense deserts? Would there be extreme heat or freezing cold? But because they knew that God was loving enough to speak to them through this new star, they also trusted that his love would bring them safely to their unknown destination.

The humility of these men is especially evident when they arrive where Mary and the child Jesus are. They immediately prostrate themselves in front of Jesus in adoration. Had they been proud they would have turned their noses up at the manger, scoffing at the idea that an august king could be born in such humble circumstances. Had they been proud they would have thought themselves better and more deserving than Mary and Jesus because of their wealth: the gold, frankincense, and myrrh that they carried. In Christianity, seeking becomes much more than an external journey; it is transformed into an inner pilgrimage. A great representative of this searching spirit is Saint Augustine. He became bishop of Hippo, a provincial town at the outposts of the Roman Empire, practically 400 years after the birth of Christ. He was spiritually awake because he never stopped searching. He was possessed by a restlessness that impelled him constantly forwards. At the beginning of his *Confessions*, that eloquent testimony to the workings of God within himself, Augustine claims that we are inherently restless because we are made for God and nothing else can satisfy us. We are propelled forward by a happy anxiety, a sense of unease with anything that is less than pure love, full perfection, and total joy, with whatever is less than God.

Wakefulness is about admitting I cannot do it on my own. A sense of dependence on God permeates the Hebrew Bible from the founding event of liberation from slavery in Egypt. The origin of Israel involved a radical upheaval of the traditional social hierarchy, an overturning that was blessed by God. This contrasts with the Greek tradition where any threat to the social order was seen as calamitous and exacted the retribution of Nemesis. In order to form the nation of Israel, God chose the most oppressed, enslaved, and degraded people in Egypt. It is evident too from the credo uttered in Deuteronomy 26:5-10, recalling the oppression in Egypt, and the gracious help of God, that the people of Israel kept the memory of their humble origins keenly alive. They were extremely vigilant about it. They were acutely grateful to God for everything they had received: deliverance from slavery, liberation from Egypt, and a new life in the Promised Land. Throughout the Hebrew Bible there is gratitude toward God; Yahweh's power is the source of their distinctiveness, of their surprising creativity, of their stubborn ability to endure despite the astonishing odds against them.[1]

Dependence on God is expressed in a more personal way by the remark in Genesis 2:7 that God formed man [*adham*] of dust from the ground [*adhama*]. Also in Latin the noun *humilitas* derives from the word for earth or soil, *humus*. Later, in Genesis 18:27, Abraham, interceding for Sodom, prefaces his request by reminding God, and more especially himself, that he is only ashes and dust, with only minimal shape and form. Deprived of the vivifying breath of God, the believer would sink back into the dust and nothingness from which he or she came (Psalm 104:29-30).

In the New Testament the Virgin Mary gives thanks to God in the *Magnificat* canticle (Luke 1:46-55) for looking upon the humility of his servant. She exalts God for the great things he does for her. But it is not as though her faith is an imagined fantasy, constructed to shield her from the demands of the real world. Her religion is not "the opium of the people," to use Marx's oft-quoted phrase. An opiate does not cure the wound; it simply dulls the pain and makes us oblivious to what is hurting us. In this sense, opium induces a comatose-like condition. But Mary is not resigned to waiting for happiness in the next life. And she refuses to see the present world as heartless or spiritless, because she is certain that God is involved in history as it is unfolding in her "now." She believes that God is about to enter history through her. Like her Jewish ancestors, she expresses the firm belief that God overturns the existing order of things.

God "has done great things for me." It is not that she proposes herself to rebel against the mighty; rather, she knows that God is already fighting on her behalf. **Wakefulness is about letting go and letting God.** Islam speaks very explicitly about humility. The Arabic word, Islam, already points to humility, for in English it means "submission" or "surrender." In fact, the first requirement of Islam is to submit oneself in complete humility before the one and only God. Without the virtue of humility, one cannot truly worship God. The Koran says that the first person to submit himself to God in this way was Abraham. He demonstrated his utter submission to God by his readiness to sacrifice his son when he thought that this was what God wanted.

A follower of Islam is called a Muslim, which in Arab means "one who surrenders to God." God is the most powerful, the Creator of all. The act of prostrating oneself to the ground during prayer is meant to be an outer sign of inward humility, a manifestation of one's lowliness and abasement before the almighty power of God. The Koran (2:43-44) tells believers, "Seek help in patience and prayer. Truly things are difficult except for the humble, those who know that they will have to meet their Lord, and that they are returning to Him." The ones who will reach paradise and live there eternally, it says, are "those who believe and do good works and humble themselves before their Lord" (11:23).

Islam, like Christianity, teaches that the sin of Satan or Iblis, as he is called, was a sin of pride. When God created Adam, He told the angels to prostrate themselves before him. Iblis refused to bow down before Adam because Adam was only fashioned from clay, whereas he was created from fire. Therefore God expelled him and he received the name "Satan." He is the one who continues to tempt believers to be arrogant and proud.

There is a saying attributed to Muhammad: "Shall I tell you about the people who belong in paradise? Everyone who is poor and humble. The people who belong in hellfire, on the other hand, are all those who are violent, cruel and arrogant."

Although the notion of surrender is not the first quality people associate with Christianity, it is nevertheless integral to Christian life. The Christian God invites unconditional surrender. This demands the humility to trust. Take the beginning of the *Spiritual Exercises* of Saint Ignatius of Loyola, a practical manual for prayer. He challenges people to start by posing some of the biggest questions in life— what am I here for? What am I going to do with the freedom entrusted to me? Ignatius himself goes straight for the jugular, proclaiming unequivocally and unapologetically what he believes the purpose of life is. According to him, human beings are here to praise, revere, and serve God in order to live with him in love forever. In a word, it is about the type of surrender that sets us free. This surrender does not damage our human dignity—far from it: it elevates our humanity. It is because human beings have such immense value in God's eyes that our Creator yearns for a loving relationship with each person, one that will have no end. Ignatius sees human life as replete with possibilities, abundant with promise and potential, pure gift. Ignatius sees an irresistible logic in using the gift to serve the Giver.

Submission and surrender are words with unhappy connotations: often they conjure up images of comatose people. We think of submissive people as those who think of themselves as inferior or accept subjugation. A person who surrenders is often thought to be a wimp, without backbone. But submission in Christian terms is the courageous decision to submit myself in absolute trust to someone I know loves me. It is *freely* deciding to make God's goals my own. And surrender is about being ready to change, to let go, to move on in life. The logic of surrender and submission is not unique to religion. It is the unwritten law of everything in the universe. Everything has a purpose to which it must submit itself if it is to be of any use. If salt can no longer fulfill its purpose of seasoning or preserving food, then it must be thrown away. If a light bulb is faulty, it can no longer supply light to illuminate a room. Human beings differ from all other creatures in that they alone can freely decide not to surrender themselves to the purpose for which they exist.

We often turn from the real purpose of life in order to concentrate our energies on making money, on providing security for ourselves, or simply in order to devote ourselves to diversion. Blaise Pascal has analyzed with uncanny insight our tragicomic attempts to run away from true happiness in order to lose ourselves in a never-ending series of short-lived gains: "We run heedlessly into the abyss after putting something in front of us to stop us seeing it."[2] This frenetic descent into the abyss is all the more unnecessary and sad, since God promises believers that if they focus their energies on his values, he will provide for their needs: "Seek first his kingdom and his righteousness, and all these things will be given to you" (Matthew 6:33). This is not just a profitable transaction; it is an incredibly generous exchange: the Christian gives his or her full attention to the lasting value of love and God takes care of everything else. The trusting person knows that God is a loving father to whom he or she can happily surrender. An honest life will bring days full of health and nights filled with sleep. And when life reaches its end, death will hold no terror. For a life lived in submission to God is immeasurably more valuable in the long term of immortality than a life of unrestrained self-assertion, however much short-term prosperity and fame the latter entails.

Wakefulness is about being grateful. In Christianity, life is seen as a marvelous gift because it is not confined to the narrow time frame separating birth and death. Despite all the evidence to the contrary, life is without end. It is a gift from God of inestimable value. Gratitude for the gift of life is not only thankfulness to God, but also to parents. After God, they are the ones to whom we most owe the gift of life. We tend to forget that the commandment to honor one's father and mother was, like all the other command-ments, addressed to adults, not to children. Of course par-ents are not perfect, though from my own experience I can-not share the pessimistic stance of Philip Larkin, whose short poem "This Be the Verse," concludes with the advice: "Get out as early as you can / And don't have any kids your-self." It is humbling to recall that my parents wiped my pos-terior clean every day for the first years of my life (though the father of a friend found this task so distasteful that he held his young son at arm's length with one hand and washed him down with the garden hose he held in the other!).

In the dialogical thought of the Jewish thinker Martin Buber there is a deep sense of gratitude to others. For Buber, it does not make sense to speak of a person in isola-tion. To be a human being is to have the capacity and the desire to enter into a direct encounter with others. The first category of being is relation. Indeed he goes so far as to claim that without the You there is no I: "Man becomes an I through a You."[3] Buber's own fragmentary autobiography portrays the self as a dynamic process, subject to re-creation and transformation through its encounters with others.[4] The story of his life shows that he had the humble gratitude to allow each I-Thou encounter to shape him anew.

Wakefulness is about knowing yourself in an honest way. The inscription engraved on the temple at Delphis in Greece said: Know yourself [*gnosthai sauton*]. Of course, knowing yourself means knowing your gifts as well as your limits. A humble person should have pride in themselves, in the best sense of that word. Positive self-knowledge is present throughout biblical writings. According to the Bible, human beings are made in the image and likeness of God; they are precious in his eyes. The Bible uses many images to convey this: God is a creator who has made us little less than gods, crowning us with glory and beauty, we are the apple of his eye, God is a mother who cherishes us as unforgettable, etc. The New Testament is adamant in asserting that all people share the dignity of being children of God. Women, slaves, and non-Jews also share in this exalted status.

Plato's great allegory of the cave shows that human beings are not initially in the light but first of all in darkness and in captivity, a humble space.[5] Even Socrates' renowned wisdom rests on an admission of ignorance: according to the *Apology*, Chaerephon, the friend of Socrates, had consulted the Delphic Oracle to discover if there was anyone alive who was wiser than Socrates. He was answered in the negative. Socrates, initially at a loss concerning the answer of the god of Delphi, went to examine a reputedly wise man in the hope of proving the oracle wrong. But he discovered otherwise. Socrates realized that his wisdom consisted in knowing his ignorance.

Pascal unites the two aspects of the self-knowledge that belong to humility. He refuses to identify the person either exclusively with greatness or merely with wretchedness. Instead of being either one or the other, the person is both great and wretched.[6] In fact, he is at pains to stress that the human being is essentially distinguished by greatness. Therefore we should not humble ourselves on account of our nature, since we were created in the image of God. Rather we should humble ourselves through contrition, since we have erred and distorted this image. The way to humility for Pascal is through replacing our self-centered vision—"the nature of self-love and of this human self is to love only self and consider only self"[7]—with a theocentric vision. Blaise Pascal offers wonderfully nuanced and eloquent descriptions in his *Pensées* of the human being as a creature that is not only derisory but also exemplary, not only one of the weakest creatures in the universe, a minuscule virus being enough to kill it, but simultaneously one of the most noble, a creature that knows its own mortality, a creature whose desires are infinite, a creature that can intellectually comprehend vast mysteries of the very universe that spatially overwhelms it.

Wakefulness is about being joyful. It is a pity Nietzsche did not meet joyful Christians. Then the German thinker would not have felt it necessary to claim that he would believe in the Redeemer if Christians actually looked redeemed. In the Bible joy leaps out between the lines, rushing to meet us in so many places, "like a bridegroom coming forth from his pavilion, like a champion rejoicing to run his course" as the nineteenth Psalm puts it. God is neither dusk nor darkness. God is pure light, high noon, the sun sending glad rays upon all. God does not sleep in a dark cavern. He leaps and bounds towards us with the urgency of love. "How beautiful on the mountains are the feet of those who bring good news" (Isaiah 52:7).

We want so much to be happy, yet we're afraid to be happy. Perhaps we fear that to be joyful is to risk exposing ourselves to pain. We do not want bliss because we do not want sadness; the two go hand in hand. We want to stay in control; we prefer this to laughing, crying, grieving, dancing. We close the shutters, protect our vulnerability and call this being together. It is self-deception. It is more enlivening to cultivate the asceticism of being joyful by risking life's ups and downs. Death is never the final word; there is always Resurrection. In the Gospel Jesus explains that we find joy to the extent that we are part of his life and his plan for humanity. If we live according to his vision of love, his joy will be in us and our joy will be complete (John 15:11).

The pervasive message about joy in the Bible is that we do not produce it ourselves. It comes from God. It is when our plans harmonize with God's plans for us that we find joy. The deeper we delve into our hearts, the more we discover that our most profound desires coincide with God's infinite desires for us. The recipe for joy is simple to understand, though not always easy to live. Although we have myriad different vocations in life, we can only find joy if we share one thing in common: service. Every one of us is called to serve others and God, whatever path we may choose. Just as Jesus washed our feet, we are invited to wash one another's feet. Whatever work we do, it should be a service to society and to God. In loving service we will find joy. If we love God with our whole heart, our whole mind, our whole soul and our whole strength, we will have everything we need, both materially and spiritually. We will have joy, the joy of leading a good life and the joy of making God happy by our love.

Wakefulness is about loving service and not loveless domination. Jesus was the kind of person that Aristotle and many other Greek and Roman thinkers would have been distinctly uneasy with. Rather than clinging to his status as God, he freely emptied himself, becoming the servant and slave of all (Philippians 2:6-8). This choice to serve was sorely tried during Jesus' temptation in the desert. Although he was God, Jesus did not thereby absolve himself from serious preparation for his ministry. He entrusted his preaching in a particular way to the Father. It was not simply a matter of a few minutes of hurried prayer in a synagogue or even an afternoon of calm meditation along the banks of the Jordan. It was forty days of prayer and of fasting in the inhospitable wilderness. Had he wanted to dominate people, he could have gone to Jerusalem and cultivated the religious authorities or the Romans. He could have taken the option that the Grand Inquisitor in *The Brothers Karamazov* berates him for not taking. But why go to people who do not believe in the immortality of the soul, to those who burden people with innumerable laws, or to the Romans who do not even believe in God? He avoided the city, the seat of religious and civic power. Nietzsche would have approved. In part three of his poetic work *Thus Spoke Zarathustra*, he gave a scathing description of a great city that was a haven for frozen spirits and limp souls, where one would gain nothing and lose everything.[8] Jesus went to a place where the human spirit is not reduced to a verbal game, in order to listen quietly to the voice of his Father that resounded with such majesty at his baptism.

Satan's temptations are serious, because he offers an effective way of making an impact. He offers guaranteed results, a "how to be successful in evangelization" program that is easy to assimilate and apply: eliminate hunger, bedazzle believers, and win the world. Of course, in each case the cost would have been the denial of the very humanity that Jesus had embraced. Rather than accepting such necessities of life as hunger, he was invited to use his divine power to bypass them by turning stones into bread. Rather than appealing to the goodness of people, he was invited to impress them with his divinity through the spectacular miracle of throwing himself from the pinnacle of the Temple. Rather than serving others, he was invited to dominate them by being the richest and most powerful person in the world.

Of course it is always easy to be wise about temptation in retrospect. We know from so many stories, songs and experiences that, however succulent the forbidden fruit may initially be, the taste turns bitter all too soon. The aftermath of any fall brings belated insight. But it is difficult to counter these blandishments in the moment they occur because of their persuasive power. It is galling for us to have to admit their compelling force, because by doing so we also confess that we have succumbed to these sweet lies many times. Fallen angel that Satan is, he has nevertheless lost little of his lucid intelligence; it is just that he dedicates this formidable intellect to nefarious ends. If Satan's insinuations were not so effective, he would not be so successful. In fact when Jesus came along, he disturbed the most lucrative enterprise in history. Until the time of Jesus, the temptation industry had enjoyed a 100% success rate.

Jesus' response to the three temptations is a magnificent illustration of his commitment to serve. There is also much to be learned from the way Satan insinuates, and the way Jesus resists, his enticements. Satan is a natural psychologist. He instinctively knows the most effective place to begin—the level of basic physical needs. Abraham Maslow's famous hierarchy of needs[9] starts at the level of physiological needs such as hunger, thirst, sleep, and bodily comforts. Only when these lower needs are satisfied can we address higher needs of security, love, esteem, and self-actualization. Maslow's hierarchy helps us to understand how a person can realize themselves, how they can be at their best. At the highest level of self-actualization the person acts out of the greatest freedom. In this encounter in the desert, we see the Adversary's hierarchy of temptations. These are ways to reduce someone to their worst, to their lowest level of freedom—enslavement to sin. The Accuser's hierarchy of temptations corresponds broadly to that of Maslow. He begins at the level of material temptations—specifically that of hunger. (And cultural temptation follows the dynamic of individual temptation—a culture first falls into a coma at the material level.) If he overcomes resistance there, it is relatively easy to progress to the emotional and spiritual levels. To maximize his chances of success, Satan times his temptations to coincide with the end of Jesus' forty days and nights of prayer and fasting—in other words, to coincide with the moment of maximum physical vulnerability.

Jesus' spirit of service is already evident in the way he reacts to the temptations. Because he is the Word of God, he responds, not with his own words, but with the Word of *God*, with the words of the Father from Deuteronomy, called *Debarim* [words] in Hebrew, to indicate that they are not only the words of Moses, but more especially the words of God. The Book of Deuteronomy is essentially a call to obedience, a call to fashion one's whole life in response to the living God who has entered history on our behalf. Jesus' first answer is a quotation from the eighth chapter of Deuteronomy, where the people are reminded of the forty years' journey through the desert. This answer of Jesus is also a prayer of praise to the God who protected the Israelites during forty years in the desert and now watches over Jesus. The following two answers are from the sixth chapter of Deuteronomy, a chapter centered on the famous *Shema* [hear] of Deuteronomy 6:4-9. For forty days Jesus has been listening to the voice of the Father speak in his soul, and now he gives a lesson in hearing and humility to the one who did not want to listen to God but only to his own proud spirit.

Jesus coped with temptation first of all by his own silence, a silence that was filled with conversation with the Father. He prayed, "Father, lead me not into temptation." (This is precisely what Eve failed to do, as we saw.) He asked the Father for help. We think we can do without God. Jesus knows the truth. The Son receives everything from the Father and the Father gives everything to the Son.

Sometimes we expect our lives as Christians to progress serenely, to be innocently free of cares, never to encounter struggles or contretemps. We do not so much want to serve God as want God to serve us. We want him to work miracles to smooth our paths, to get rid of the angled cobblestones. Sometimes that happens, but at times we are also called to love when faced with hatred, to remain dependent on God when offered the independence of wealth and power, to be chaste when sensual indulgence beckons. Jesus' example teaches us that to be humble is to empty ourselves of what is inessential, and to guard fiercely what is essential—a deep sense of our dependence upon God, complete surrender to him, and selfless service.

As this chapter draws to a close, I realize that I have drawn most of my examples from Christianity. I guess someone could retort, "it is easy to talk about signs of wakefulness when you are drawing on so many religious sources, not to mention philosophers whose ideas are in sympathy with the Christian world view. But when it comes to the world we are living in today, does this religious rhetoric really cut any ice?" That is why in the next chapter I want to switch gears and draw on a gifted contemporary writer who does not have a specifically Christian agenda, just to see if he too is homing in on this comatose state of ours.

5

A Secular Wake-up Call

But we had stopped caring, and that's a fact. We knew our days were numbered. We had fouled our lives and we were getting ready for a shake-up.
Raymond Carver, "Gazebo"

So far we have seen how humility, although not always the most admired human disposition, is nevertheless crucial. We have caught glimpses of our spiritual drowsiness and have identified the sin of Adam and Eve as the point where the stupor set in. We have looked at an example of a way out of the coma that does not lead anywhere, because it trusts too much in human power. We have seen possibilities of waking up to a mystery that surpasses us and a grace that embraces us. We have gone through a checklist to see how wakeful we are: ticking off items such as awareness, gratitude, surrender, honest self-knowledge, joy, and loving service. But can these signs of wakefulness find a home in our secularized world? After all, our culture is not exactly crazy about things like service, surrender, thankfulness, and honesty.

If I am having a bad day and I look at our culture, things do not seem so promising. There is an unending series of problems, from the mounting bankruptcy of individualism to the warlike stance reflected in our failure to observe the undemanding dictates of courtesy; we are even threatened with the loss of belief in morality itself. But our comatose state is neither permanent nor irreversible. Certainly, a lot of big things are wrong. But there are also many encouraging little things, unreported in the large-scale chronicle that is history. The latter belongs to the victors. But the little stories we weave every day deserve attention. They even merit celebration. The good little things that happen might not seem world-shattering, but who said that tiny seeds of hope cannot mushroom?

Take the twentieth century secularist writer Raymond Carver.[1] If I chose an explicitly religious short story writer like Flannery O'Connor, someone could rightly say that, considering the Christian hope that already suffuses her stories, I am ultimately discovering nothing, just confirming what is already there—which is not at all a bad thing, by the way! But with Carver, it is different: he does not write with an explicitly Christian purpose. However, the more you read his stories, the more you realize how wonderfully warm and human he is. It doesn't leap out of the pages at you; but it is still there, a hidden pearl buried in a sparsely yet carefully cultivated field.

Carver's short stories are full of working class Americans who lead bleak and broken lives at the periphery of society, at the difficult edges of relationships, at the dark side of hope. Yet there is something ennobling in the way his short stories approach otherwise pathetic lives. He elevates these characters because of his own humility. Raymond Carver was transparently and unselfconsciously humble at a personal level. His stories show that he is also humble in his use of language. He has a living sense of the sacredness of words; indeed, he is often so circumspect with words that there is a profound silence at the heart of many of his stories. This silence is also a silence about others, an expression of respect that prevents the narrator from supposing that he can delve too deeply into their lives. In one of his stories "Put Yourself In My Shoes," the protagonist, a struggling writer called Myers, is told by a neighbor that he could write an excellent story if only he could somehow get inside the head of a local university lecturer who has had a passionate affair with a female student. Later the same neighbor tells Myers that he is not a writer because he does not try to understand people enough to get inside their skins. Carver tells that story with a twinkle in his eye, because he respects people so much that he refuses to stand steadily in their shoes; he offers only glimpses and snatches of their inner lives.

What is most striking about Carver's short stories is that they are not so much about figuring out the lives of his characters as they are about helping the reader to understand his or her own life better. In other words, his stories highlight our comatose state and show that waking up, although difficult, is not impossible. In his harrowing and emotionally charged story "So Much Water So Close To Home," a wife called Claire identifies with a girl whose naked body has been found floating in a river by Claire's husband Stuart and some friends during a fishing trip. Stuart and his friends had discovered the body on a Friday evening but, not wanting to interrupt their fishing trip, one of them tied the girl's wrist to some tree roots at the shore, and they all continued fishing until Sunday afternoon. Claire pictures these family men drinking whiskey, exchanging crude stories, and washing their dishes in the water, all the while just a matter of yards away from this unfortunate girl. Later the autopsy shows that the girl was raped and then strangled. Claire can see the girl's tragedy in embryonic form in her own life, in the manner in which her husband relates to her as an object, in the way she notices other men looking at her body. Her husband tries to repair the damage in their relationship by offering her sex, whereas what she wants is reverence, or at least respect. The more she imaginatively identifies with the girl the more she withdraws from Stuart as an unnamed illness she had a number of years before once again threatens to submerge her. There is still a relationship between husband and wife at the end of the story, but new rules will have to be agreed upon.

The people Carver looks at are not important in the eyes of the world, but he makes them so. He sees the dignity that they often find so difficult to identify themselves. They are either unemployed or hold down insignificant jobs. Their personal lives are confused and bewildered. Sometimes there is a barely perceptible stirring toward hope, toward others, toward putting the desperate jigsaw of daily life into some rudimentary order. The ray of sunlight in the distance is never unambiguously bright; it could also herald the beginning of a long-term eclipse; the light at the end of the tunnel could be the headlights of an oncoming train. In an early short story, "The Student's Wife," a woman has trouble sleeping. This awakens a deeper grief, one she cannot name or put her finger on. She and her husband talk about the past, but the memories they recall only serve to pull them further apart. She gets up and witnesses a sunrise that does not carry any hope. On the contrary, it is full of menace and foreboding; she finds herself tightening her robe as the cold dampness seeps into her. When she returns to the bedroom, her husband looks wild in his sleep, his jaws shut tightly and one of his arms occupying her side of the bed. She gets down on her knees and the story ends with her heartfelt and desperate prayer: "'God,' she said. 'God, will you help us, God?' she said."[2]

Our contemporary landscape often does not show us the possibilities of waking up; it seeks to comfort us instead, in the knowledge that others are even more spiritually dead than we are. *The Jerry Springer Show* gladly succumbs to the temptation that Carver studiously avoids—to look down on its cast of characters, to despise them, to elevate itself and its viewers through cheapening those who are discarded after their short-lived collision with fame. The show gives the thumbs up to pride if it is unabashed and aggressive. It is acceptable to cheat on your wife if you do it with a swagger. But meekness and humility will only earn you the ridicule of the studio audience. Raymond Carver and Jerry Springer focus on the same constituency, the American underclass. The former values them enough to focus all his writing upon their elevation. The latter lowers them to trailer trash, a diverting and freakish spectacle. People who hate each other are seated a couple of feet apart on this TV show and are asked provocative questions to encourage them to attack one another. The audience gets great entertainment out of the violence and the bizarre relationships of the guests. They are reassured that these weirdos and freaks are not mainstream and normal, unlike themselves.

Carver, however, shows us the links between his characters and our own stories. Maybe the circumstances of our lives are more fortunate, but there are still anguished questions, wounds, painful memories, and fearful relationships. Carver empties himself as he faithfully records the brokenness in ordinary lives. He does not presume to offer grand explanations of a psychological or sociological kind for the behavior he barely describes. He is not pushing any new theories, he is not a covert sociologist. He simply offers spare descriptions, as minimal as the brushstrokes of Oriental calligraphy. But even though he does not waste words, he makes it clear that the lives of his characters are threatening to disintegrate. Sadly for these hurting people, they lack the vocabulary to name their problems. They are so emotionally poor that they do not know what is eating away at their lives. When you cannot name the problem that aggravates you, it ends up weighing you down even more. But Carver does allow his characters to make some kind of sense of their lives, however brittle it may be. They catch a glimpse of their own anguish reflected in the lives of others and because of that their own lives become just a little less bewildering. Carver's world does not have the sure confidence and unbreakable hope of Easter. There are no dramatic Resurrections. It is a secular world bereft of supernatural assistance. But there is a grittiness about these characters: somehow they keep struggling. You have to admire their endurance, the fact that despite all the pain, they get on with their precarious lives. And these fragile lives are graced with a sliver of hope.

Carver, for all his uncomfortable realism, is a hopeful writer. Like John-Paul Sartre, the French existentialist, Carver experienced and saw his fair share of hardships. In fact, given Carver's difficult economic circumstances, he probably had less time and leisure than Sartre to theorize or to reflect on the vicissitudes of life. Yet unlike Sartre,

Carver does not despair of other people. Sartre's reflections lead him to a very pessimistic conclusion. The character Garcin makes the celebrated comment "hell is other people" in Scene 5 of *No Exit*. It is an assertion that dovetails neatly with Sartre's philosophy, where the other person constantly threatens the self's proud position of domineering freedom. When the other person gazes at the self, this sovereign subject now finds that he or she has been reduced to an object in the other's eyes, and this is intolerable. Thereafter, life becomes a battlefield for domination and mastery. But Carver, although he is aware of the cut-throat nature of society, does not see things in such a dark manner. He refuses to be ground down by life's hassles.

Neither did Levinas become disheartened, even though he went through more painful experiences than Sartre during the Second World War—five years as a prisoner in a military camp in Germany, not to mention the cruel loss of his family. Despite the trauma he endured, Levinas managed to see the other person as a heavenly invitation rather than a hellish threat. He saw life as a call to respond to the other. It was the other person who came first. "As the Bible says: 'He who loses his soul gains it.' The ethical I is a being who asks if he has a right to be, who excuses himself to the other for his own existence."[3]

And this other is forever elusive, according to Levinas. The endeavor to safeguard otherness is an enterprise "of great pitch and moment" for Levinas. It is his way of keeping the self awake, for when I reduce the other to something I can know and control, I slide into a coma. When it comes to the ethical encounter with the other, Levinas believes it is erroneous and potentially catastrophic to presume that the self and the other are two of a kind. Levinas' position goes against our common-sense understanding of ourselves and of others. Indeed it seems to abandon common sense altogether. What is the point of insisting on this absolute difference between the other and me? We can certainly accept relative differences—witness the success of John Gray's book *Men Are From Mars, Women Are From Venus*. But whatever planet someone may be from, can we not at least call them another person? They may communicate differently, exhibit different emotional needs, and behave unlike us, but aren't they still human beings? Why is it so misguided and dangerous to talk of another as another man or another woman? Certainly it makes sense when we are formulating laws, carrying out scientific observations, practicing medicine, and so on. There are so many professional and social activities that simply would not function if we did not speak of others as other human beings, as other men and women. But when it comes to the unique situation of encountering someone in all their mystery, it can often be best to leave our labels and our categories aside.

Both Raymond Carver and Emmanuel Levinas show a deep respect for other people. By doing so they echo the enormous reverence that God has for every human being. When it comes to respecting other people, God's heart is so immense that there is room in it for everybody as though each were the only one. In fact each person is so special in the eyes of God that he would have sent his Son to save that one person alone. What makes each person unique is the divine part inside that comes from the true God. This living gem is the soul, and it bears an altogether individual stamp in each person. Being in the image of God is not a question of visual similarity: if it were, then Nicole Kidman's beauty would reflect God more faithfully than Mother Teresa of

Calcutta's goodness. But in fact we have elevated the beautiful, rich and powerful to the status of at least minor divinities. It is obvious that our everyday notions of true humanity and real divinity need to be purified. That is why we need to remind ourselves that the image of God within is not beautified by fame or wealth; instead it glows when it is nourished with divine things—with love, with peace, with truth. It is only doing what is evil that can wound or kill the soul, depriving it of the peace that love brings.

Of course the soul does not become beautiful overnight. Neither does it descend into ugliness all of a sudden. It takes patience and time to embellish the life of the soul. The ascent to goodness and the descent to evil are both gradual, and prepared for by many small decisions and choices. The soul does not descend into a serious coma without steady corruption through bad habits. Certainly anyone is capable of doing something really evil on the spur of the moment, something that can throw them completely off balance spiritually. Yet because their heart still has spaces of freedom inside, it will be possible for them to get up again, although bruised and shaken.

If we could see the soul that sinks into lifelessness it would not be a pretty sight. It would look dehydrated and parched. The prophet Ezekiel had a harrowing vision of dry bones. When people no longer have the life of the spirit within them, they are like the dry bones that Ezekiel saw; they are like lifeless corpses. Why do people dry up? Why do their spirits fall asleep when they are surrounded by opportunities to live and to love? Why do they walk away from the living waters in order to die in the parched desert? These are questions that only each person can ultimately answer. Jesus offers the most hopeful and invigorating answer of all. He draws people to himself, allowing them to imbibe deeply from the wellsprings of his spirit, so that they may drink and never be thirsty again. Only Jesus is "Other" in the extraordinary way that he can confidently issue such an astonishing invitation.

We sometimes say that the face is the window of the soul. I think this is true above all in the case of Jesus. He was "full of grace and truth," as John 1:14 puts it. In the next chapter I want to behold the face of Jesus; I want to see how that face, in the moments of intense suffering when it was apparently most wounded and deformed, was in fact the very life that can awaken our culture from its sluggish sleep.

6

The Face that Wakes Us Up

*Then something like a smile passed fleetingly over
what had once been her face.*

Anna Akhmatova,
"Instead of a Preface" from "Requiem"

We tend to interpret a person's character from his or her
face. If that were not so, many advertisers, filmmakers, and
caricaturists would be out of a job. When serial killers and
mass murderers are apprehended, people often express surprise that they look so normal. Lady Macbeth warned her
husband that his face revealed his wickedness too readily:
"Your face, my Thane, is as a book where men may read
strange matters" (*Macbeth*, Act 1, Scene 5). Other
Shakespearean characters were more successful at disguise.
It was only through the ghost of his dead father that Hamlet
realized his uncle Claudius was not all he pretended to be:
"That one may smile, and smile, and be a villain" (*Hamlet*,
Act 1, Scene 5). Richard III, Duke of Gloucester, furthered
his ambitions for the crown while concealing them with creative forms of facial dissimulation. He resolved to "wet my
cheeks with artificial tears / and frame my face for all occasions" (*King Henry VI, Part III*, Act 3, Scene 2).

Lady Macbeth, Claudius, and the Duke of Gloucester were all intent on turning the face into a mask. We can use our faces as masks in order to give others a particular impression of ourselves or sometimes to refuse them any distinct impression. We can attempt to manipulate or dictate their reactions to us, mostly to engineer a favorable reaction to ourselves. Our faces can give impressions in various ways: we can adopt a happy or sad expression, we can narrow our eyes or set our mouth into a fixed grimace. Above all it is from our faces that spoken language emerges—we talk and engage others in conversation.

Although the face as a mask figures prominently in these three Shakespearean plays, in the Bible the face is most often understood differently—not as a mask, but as a true revelation of the person. The Hebrew word *p nîm* appears more than two thousand times in different forms throughout the Hebrew Bible to denote the word "face." Because the face reveals the person, the Bible is insistent that the face of God never appears. Otherwise God's mystery and transcendence would be compromised. *Exodus* 33:20 makes it clear that nobody can see God's face and live. The face, then, is more than something external.

It was this Biblical background that inspired Levinas to go beyond a visual perspective in discussing the face. When he invites us to reflect on the face in an ethical context, he does not want us to scrutinize it as a way of sizing up character. Neither is he interested in drawing attention to features such as the length of the nose or the shape of the eyes or the width of the mouth. He believes that these ways of observing the face can lead us to treat the other as an object. Although he recognizes that our culture relates to the face in a perceptual mode, he is convinced that this approach does not bring us to the essence of what the face is. He wants to go beyond the face as mask. Essential to the face is its vulnerability, its exposure, its lack of defense. We realize the poverty of the face when we notice how people try to conceal this deprivation by putting on a mask, by preparing "a face to meet the faces that you meet" (T.S. Eliot, "The Love Song of J. Alfred Prufrock").

Although a person's eyes can be especially expressive, when it comes to the face, Levinas is interested more in the ears and mouth than in the eyes. In other words, he is fascinated by the fact that we speak with the mouth and hear with the ears. This is partly due to his Jewish upbringing.[1] Levinas is influenced by the insistence on hearing in the Jewish tradition. To take a single, albeit crucial, example: The recitation enjoined upon Jews in *Deuteronomy* 6:4-9, begins with the words "Hear O Israel" [*Shema Israel*]. Over time the *Shema* became the central Jewish confession of faith. This prayer is to be recited aloud daily, so that the believer appropriates the words, so that they become his or her own, so that no part of his or her being can escape the call. The command articulated in this prayer challenges the way of being of the Hebrew people; it invites them to transcend themselves. In the midst of a life where so many secondary and corrupt words are heard, this word is intended to become primary as it purifies the person through repetition.

Why the resistance to vision in Levinas? Because vision tends to make me the center of everything. It as though everything else exists for my sake, as though all things were there simply in order to give themselves to me. I can be tempted to imagine the world as my world, a world I possess and control. It becomes subordinate to me. If this sounds a little abstract, just reflect a moment on the tradi tional Christian teaching about modesty of the eyes. It is because Christians realized how possessive sight and vision could be that they encouraged people to be careful in what they set their eyes on. Since vision is inclined to claim ownership, the eye that sees a beautiful body wants to possess it. The eye that lingers on the wealth of the rich wants to acquire this wealth as well. The eye that is transfixed by power seeks it too. Therefore control of vision will lead to control of the powerful drives fueled by sight.

The theologian Hans Urs von Balthasar has written a marvelous article comparing the senses of seeing and hearing.[2] It complements Levinas' in a wonderfully articulate way. According to von Balthasar the eye enables us to comprehend, dominate, possess, subordinate, and encompass the world. It is distinguished from the other senses by the fact that it needs separation from its objects in order to see them. It controls objects precisely through this distance, like a trainer taming animals in a circus ring. Even when we enter a beautiful landscape, which extends to the furthest horizons, and wander through it, we can never actually enter the picture itself, so to speak. When it is a matter of human beings, only those who are equal can gaze into one another's eyes. If there is inequality, one person lowers the eyes or hides or becomes stiff. There is also a spiritual seeing, though it is always seeing through a mirror or through a glass darkly, as Saint Paul wrote. Fundamentally all seeing on earth is a seeing that does not truly see. Although Jesus is the revelation of the Father, Saint John nevertheless proclaims that "no one has ever seen God." Yet the ultimate goal is a face to face encounter, a seeing where we "shall know even as we are known." Von Balthasar identifies the Orthodox Church with this Johannine aspiration towards total seeing. It aims at the immediate encounter with God; its ultimate goal is deification. If there is a possible weakness in this perspective, it is that of identifying with God to such an extent that one negates the world. This happens if the inherent dynamic of seeing is taken to its ultimate extent.

The sense of hearing contrasts with that of seeing in several ways. We only need to recall the fact that we hear in the dark to realize that we do not actually hear objects themselves. Rather, we hear what they utter or communicate. As a rule we are not the ones who decide what should be put before us to hear and when it should be put there. That which we hear arrives without letting us know beforehand, and takes our attention without prior permission, like the mobile phone that rings impertinently in our pocket. Von Balthasar therefore sees something deeply symbolic in the fact that our eyes have lids, but not our ears. He also notes that since sound travels more slowly than light waves, we instinctively realize that what we hear has already finished before it arrives, and so we no longer have control over it. The voice we hear, which is at once invisible and full of presence, mediates mystery. The communication is mysterious because sound only transmits the utterance. It does not communicate the being who utters. Von Balthasar compares speaking to an arrow that enters into us more deeply than any look could do, but adds that the bow from which the arrow is shot does not come into our possession. Hearing oscillates between revelation and mystery because even when a being tries to express itself fully, it is fundamentally unable to do so. Neither is there equality between speaker and hearer since in the moment of hearing the hearer is in the humble position of receiving and belongs to the other in obedience.

In spiritual hearing we are obliged to await God's voice passively. We never possess him as an object within ourselves. We hear God as indistinct yet alluring music in the midst of the din of the world. When the Christian community speaks God's word, it must be simultaneously listening to that word itself. Hearing is of the utmost importance spiritually since "faith comes from hearing." At the Transfiguration of Jesus, the sound of the Father's voice is heard, commanding the apostles to listen to his beloved Son. The humility of hearing will only be deepened in eternity: "the act of hearing aims upward into an ever more perfect obedience and thus into a creatureliness that distinguishes itself ever more humbly from the Creator. This humility will not be abolished in eternity, because the truth of the relationship between God and man expresses itself ever more perfectly in it."[3]

Von Balthasar identifies the Western Church with the spiritual sense of hearing. It listens obediently and humbly to God's word, and it reaches towards the world in proclaiming this word. It does not seek to become blind to the world through living more and more in the light of God's presence. Instead it seeks to pay homage to God by serving the world. The Western Church falls into two heresies, according to von Balthasar. First of all, it devotes itself so exclusively to the word that it closes itself to the objective and visible meaning of this word that is spoken to it. Secondly, it becomes so immersed in the world it is serving that it stops listening to the word it is supposed to preach. The distinction between seeing and hearing enables von Balthasar to situate all the Christian Churches along a spectrum of sight and sound—"between Athos and Wittenberg, pure vision and pure hearing."[4]

Levinas sees how the defenselessness of the face is ambiguous. Although its very weakness cries out to us not be violent, it is precisely the same exposedness that make it so vulnerable to violence. In the passion and death of his fellow Jew Jesus, we find an absolutely harrowing example of this. A disfigured face is one we instinctively turn away from. Such is the face of Jesus in His final hours on earth. It is a face, as Isaiah 53 announces prophetically, that is without beauty or majesty. Jesus allows human beings to reduce him to this humiliated condition where he looks like a leper, like one cursed by God and of no account. And yet it is precisely in these moments when Jesus seems so much less than human, so reduced in dignity, that he is achieving the work of waking *us* up from our inhumane condition.

I would like to offer a few brief reflections that could help convey something of the history of the face of Jesus from the moment of his betrayal to the moment of his death. This enterprise is doomed from the outset because it is impossible to describe these hours in an even remotely adequate way. The Gospels themselves give us only the bare outline of the passion of Jesus. They say too little rather than too much. As John tells us at the end of his own Gospel, were everything about Jesus' life to be told, the world itself could not contain the books that would have to be written. In the absence of a lot of hard facts, I will be giving a certain freedom of rein to my imagination. But in fleshing out the skeletal summary offered by the evangelists, I want to present a portrait that is more than simply fanciful. I will try to keep my remarks faithful to the spirit of the Gospels.

Jesus' face is first kissed by a traitor. "Judas, are you betraying the Son of Man with a kiss?" (Luke 22:48) This must be the most painful kiss ever endured. An analogy: A good guitarist has a heightened sensitivity to guitars that are out of tune, to incorrect chords, and so on. In a similar way, Jesus is the one who has the most exquisite sensibility where love is concerned. And so this betrayal of love, although not manifesting itself in a visible wound, must sear his heart. Judas uses a universal sign of intimacy and friendship to betray Jesus. This is truly a murderous kiss, one that will lead to the death of Jesus and to the death of a friendship he has offered with generosity and with ever-increasing pain to Judas. Its deceit lacerates Jesus' heart, hacking through his finest feelings with brutal disregard. We have talked about the invisibility of the face in Levinas. In the case of this hypocritical kiss, we can speak of the invisibility of a wound that cuts deeper emotionally than any physical wound ever could. "If an enemy were insulting me, I could endure it . . . But it is you, a man like myself, my companion, my close friend!" (Psalm 55:12-14)

The Gospel of Luke tells us that the guards who had custody of Jesus mocked him and struck him, blindfolding him, asking him to guess who had hit him (Luke 22:63-64). The next morning Jesus is brought before Pilate who, after questioning him, finds him innocent. Pilate offers to release Jesus and instead tries to appease the crowd by offering to execute the known murderer and revolutionary Barabbas (Mark 15:9). But instead of crying for the release of the real son of the father, Jesus, the crowds want a bogus one released—Barabbas, "son of the father" [abba]. Pilate decides to subject Jesus to the most severe form of the three grades of physical punishment used by the

Romans—scourging [*verberatio*], hoping in this way to placate the crowd's anger, and have him freed. From references to other incidents of scourging in the writings of such contemporary authors as Josephus we know that it was a particularly harsh lashing, often ripping off large chunks of flesh and exposing the bone, slicing nerves, in some cases leading to death. Presumably, Pilate wanted to show the crowd that he was ready to have Jesus beaten almost to death so that afterwards the mob would not want him executed. The scourging was generally applied with leather straps fitted with pieces of metal or bone at the end. It is most likely that no part of his body was spared. The damage to his face would have been dreadful. The blows would have split open the thin layer of skin on his face, blood would have poured out, and the repeated blows would have caused extreme pain to the myriad fresh wounds. At the end of the scourging his face would have been so bloody and bruised that it would have appeared to be one big purple and blue sore. Trying to reconstruct a face after such maltreatment would be a nightmare for a plastic surgeon of today.

After the scourging, Jesus was crowned with thorns. Our image of this is falsified by the many statues and paintings where the crown forms a smooth and symmetrical pattern, a perfect circle. The soldiers had no intention of creating an artistic masterpiece. They simply cut some thorns from a nearby bush, forced them into an untidy wreath and pressed the crown into Jesus' head. It is almost certain that they did not get the dimensions of the crown right the first time. They either had to cut some thorns off when the crown was already on his head, also wounding Jesus in the process, or else they had to tear it off his head to adjust the size, before forcing it down once again, this time in a different position, opening new wounds, no doubt piercing the nape of his neck and forehead, but possibly even one or both eyes.

They dressed him in a purple garment, put a reed in his hand, mocking him and spitting at him. Pilate had him placed before the crowd. "Here is the man!" (John 19:5) The rabble saw a woebegone face, his hair and beard matted and tangled with a mixture of blood, spittle and sweat. Having been scourged, slapped, punched, cut, his head was spinning, his ears ringing, his eyes bruised black and blue, his nose swollen. "All who see me mock me; they hurl insults, shaking their heads" (Psalm 22:7).

A roughly cut beam was hoisted onto Jesus' back and he made his way haltingly to Calvary. At this stage his eyes were probably encrusted with blood, his lips bruised and split, the hair on his head and beard torn away in places. Bystanders no doubt hurled stones and lumps of earth at his face. When he fell on the rocky path, pebbles and dirt would have become embedded into his blood-soaked face. When he arrived at the place of crucifixion, his mother must have stifled a scream when she saw that beloved face twisted and tortured almost beyond recognition.

Jesus would have been shoved roughly onto the horizontal cross as workmen nailed him to it. As it was raised and lowered into the hole prepared for it, the cross would have swayed precariously, Jesus' body and face jolting forward, only to hit back against the wood, hammering the thorns once again into his head and face. His eyes could barely see the few friends before him. All around were blurred and shifting images of soldiers and a contemptuous mob. His ears, clogged with blood, could dimly hear a continuous din as the crowd uttered their blasphemies and abuse. Closer to Jesus there was a loud and incessant buzzing as swarms of flies and other insects converged around their prey, sucking at his blood as if he were a piece of discarded flesh, blackening whole areas of his face and body.

Eventually he breathes his last. He has shrunk from our sight. There is silence. He is something from which we turn our eyes. The resonant voice has long since disappeared. He is dumb, a lamb who has been led to the slaughter. The handsome countenance is no more. There is no majesty to draw our eyes. The composed, serene expression that was his is now a distant memory. There is no grace that would make us delight in him. And yet there is a mysterious beauty in this face, even though we may hold him of no account, because it is a face that saves us, much more so than the striking and virile face of Jesus' life.

What message is revealed and concealed in the tortured face of Jesus? Fundamentally, this disfigured face is the greatest manifestation of God in our world. God reveals himself best in this face that has lost the semblance of any human one. To the eyes of any onlooker there is no divine omnipotence here. How then can we recognize the features of divinity in the countenance of Christ? How is this not just a tragedy of human dimensions? It is love that convinces. Jesus is love. He is not denying his divinity by this utter self-abasement, but confirming it to the highest degree, in this foolish generosity that impels him to complete self-surrender. This is where his divinity is both concealed and revealed.

Jesus' very face has buckled at the unimaginable pressure exerted by the meeting of perfect self-giving love with the hateful "no" of human beings. Because Jesus does not rely on divine power to save him—as he explained to his captors at Gethsemane, he could have had more than twelve legions of angels to defend him had he asked the Father—what we also see here is humanity at its fullest. Paradoxically, this despised face is the face of someone who is more, not less, human than we are. This disfigured face is now, in fact, the litmus test for all faces. There is a mysterious truth hidden in its ugliness.

The onlookers without faith judged this bruised and battered faith from the perspective of their own supposedly normal and relatively pain-free faces. Therefore they became even more convinced of its irrelevance and offensiveness, rejecting it and spitting upon it. But we are invited to behold this face in a different way. We are asked to adore it, so that it now becomes the point of departure from which we evaluate our own faces, our own emotional and spiritual engagement. My love, my life, and the choices I make and pursue are now judged in the light of this weakest and most suffering face of all. But precisely because of the utter defenselessness of that face, this judgment is not severe. The deeds that have been committed in hatred of this face are more than harsh. But the face itself gives a judgment that is nothing but mercy and compassion. And here we once again encounter compelling evidence of its divinity. What other face could respond to barbarism with such an incredible amount of mercy and meekness? Only the face of the most innocent lamb that remains mute as it is led to the slaughter.

I began this chapter with a quote from the great Russian poet Anna Akhmatova. It comes from the prose preface to her poetical sequence entitled "Requiem," which was written between the years 1935 and 1940 but was not published in the Soviet Union until 1987. In 1957 she added "Instead of a Preface" from which the citation at the start of this chapter is taken.[5] In these short and moving lines she describes how for seventeen months during the Yezhov terror, she stood in line practically every day outside the prison in Leningrad. In 1936 Stalin had appointed Nikolai Yezhov head of the People's Commissariat for Internal Affairs (NKVD). As chief of the secret police, Yezhov was in charge of the big purges of 1938, during which Anna's only son Lev was arrested. She used to stand silently along with the other women, since they were all afraid that there might be informers in the queue. One day as she lined up outside the blind prison wall, hoping for news of her son's fate and perhaps clutching a parcel of bread for him, somebody in the crowd recognized her as the poet Anna Akhmatova. This awoke a glimmer of hope in the woman behind her, who whispered to Anna, asking her to write about this humiliating experience, so that the suffering of all these women waiting to hear of their sons, husbands, brothers, and fathers might not sink without trace into the brutally anonymous currents of Stalinist history. The poor woman was looking for a ray of light in the darkness, she was desperate for some crumbs of comfort and meaning in the midst of so much numbing horror. And when Anna assured her that she could describe the indescribable, that she would be a witness to this ghastly episode of history, a ghostly image of a smile momentarily lit up the space where the woman's face had once been. At the end of history a great shroud will be woven full of faces such as this, and we will be judged by how we helped to restore a smile to bluish lips and warmth to frozen eyes.

However moving the loving face of Jesus may be, it is not always welcomed by hearts. He does not live up to all our expectations. Jesus does not struggle with the mighty in order to establish any earthly empire or political superpower. He will not fulfill all our power-hungry ambitions. Rather he combats the power of darkness. He wants to break the chains of evil. But he has a deep reverence for our freedom: if someone is intent on remaining enslaved, then so be it.

7

Alive or Comatose – John or Judas?

*One of them, the disciple whom Jesus loved, was
reclining next to him.*

(John 13:23)

Although people can fall into physical comas quite suddenly, we do not descend into spiritual comas overnight. They
take much more time. And they demand the active consent
of the person involved. In this chapter I want to look at the
actions and decisions of Judas Iscariot that steadily dragged
him into a spiritually comatose state. I want to contrast him
with his fellow apostle John. If John was humble, then
Judas was proud. Yet these two men with such diverse des-
tinies lived and ministered side by side for three years.

Let me say in advance that although I will be pointing
to a descending spiral of evil actions in the case of Judas, I
am not making any judgement about his eternal fate. I
believe that hell exists, but taking my cue from Pope John
Paul II, I am not claiming that Judas is necessarily there.
"Even when Jesus says of Judas, the traitor 'it would have
been better for that man if he had never been born' (Mt.
26:24), his words do not allude for certain to eternal damnation."[1]

In describing both John and Judas, I will rely principally on the Gospel of John. Great minds, among them C.H. Dodd, Raymond Brown, and Rudolf Schackenburg, have examined this Gospel in exhaustive detail; every week new articles and monographs appear on diverse aspects of the Johannine writings. But to adapt a phrase of Pascal, sometimes the God of the scripture scholars is not the God of Abraham, Isaac, and Jacob. The questions explored by many scholars undoubtedly shed valuable light on John's Gospel. But this illumination is above all the light of reason, which is only a partial light and at times a distorting one. Reason is partial because it can never satisfactorily elucidate such mysteries as the Word becoming flesh or the Resurrection. Reason is a distorting instrument because it reflects the historical ways of thinking of human beings, and thus is inevitably subject to fallibility and bias.

In the *Concluding Unscientific Postscript*, Søren Kierkegaard, writing under the pseudonym Johannes Climacus,[2] helps guard us against being overwhelmed by this proliferation of biblical scholarship. He introduces a helpful distinction between an objective inquiry about the truth value of Christianity and a subjective inquiry into the relationship of the person to Christianity.[3] The former is a "what" question—for instance, what are the scriptures, what can we assert in their regard? The second is a "how" question—how is scripture going to affect me, how am I to live? Scripture scholars are engaged in an objective understanding of biblical texts, their sources, structure, language, sociological milieu, and so on. This objective approach is of course not just useful in the purely conceptual sphere: the results of excellent research can nourish our faith and inspire our actions. But the disadvantage of this formidable erudition is that the object of its investigation, the scriptural texts, are essentially focused on encouraging people to live in an excellent manner rather than merely to understand in a rational way. The truth of the Bible is essentially a saving truth, the purpose of which is to change our hearts and to train us in righteousness. (See 2 Timothy 3:14-17.) To the extent that they neglect or minimize the central core of the Bible as an ethico-religious message and prioritize instead the purely cognitive level, scripture scholars betray the Bible by ignoring or minimizing the very reason for which it is so vital to Christians—because it offers them a message that saves.

It is obvious that I have some reservations about biblical scholarship. But I make these remarks not to denigrate the valuable work of scripture scholars but rather to offer some justification for my own manner of interpreting John's Gospel. My interpretation is guided above all by the conviction that there is a saving message of infinite value at stake, and that this merits passionate interest. I do not discount the rich findings of scholarship.[4] My purpose is to stimulate thinking on what it means to be a humble and wakeful disciple. But first, a few words about the authorship of the Gospel of John.

Scripture scholars have many different theories concerning the author or authors of John's Gospel. I believe it was written by an apostle, and I believe that this apostle was John. Only an apostle would have been privy to the questions, reactions, and misunderstandings of fellow apostles described at various stages in the Gospel. Moreover, if an apostle were not the author of the Gospel, it would be difficult to explain how someone more distant from Jesus could be aware of Jesus' inner thoughts at crucial times—for example, when we are told at the beginning of the Last Supper that Jesus knew his hour had arrived to pass from this world to the Father.

There is nothing far-fetched about the claim that the apostle in question was John. By asserting it, I trust the evidence of witnesses of the time, the evidence of the text, the evidence supplied by the author's intimate familiarity with Jesus' thoughts, with the disciples' reactions, with the customs of early first century Palestine, and more. I find the evidence of near contemporaries compelling. For instance, Irenaeus, the famous second century theologian and saint, declared that the author was John himself. Eusebius informs us that Irenaeus would have known this through Polycarp, who was a direct disciple of John. In fact it was John himself who appointed Polycarp head of the Church in Smyrna. Irenaeus writes that as a boy at Smyrna, he heard Polycarp recount stories about John and other people close to Jesus. Thus we have a direct and unbroken line from John to Irenaeus. All the major Church Fathers trusted Irenaeus' conviction that the fourth gospel was the work of John.

There is also corroboration in the text itself. In the penultimate sentence of the Gospel, the author identifies himself as the beloved disciple (John 21:24). After recounting the crucifixion of Christ, the author of the Gospel stresses that he himself saw what he is witnessing about (John 19:35). Admittedly, even if the author of the Gospel is the beloved disciple, this does not necessarily prove that he is John. In fact, certain scholars reject the identification of the beloved disciple with John. But there is evidence to the contrary. It makes sense that this beloved disciple is John if we put the following facts side by side. First, the other Gospels confirm that the apostle John was especially close to Jesus.

Second, in the thirteenth chapter of John's Gospel, Peter asks the beloved disciple, who is sitting next to Jesus, to ask who the traitor is. In terms of inductive logic or analogical reasoning, the conclusion I am suggesting (that John is the beloved disciple) does not of course follow necessarily from the premises, but is nevertheless probable.

The apostle John is close to Jesus; the beloved disciple, resting against the heart of Jesus, is close (not only spatially!) to Jesus; so the apostle John is likely to be the beloved disciple.

While the conclusion is by no means watertight from a logical point of view, since John is not the *only* one close to Jesus—Peter and James also are—it is highly probable.

Let us turn now to the figure of John (from the Hebrew *Yôhanan*, meaning "God has been gracious"), the Beloved Disciple. In the Prologue to his Gospel, the author John tells us that John the Baptist is a witness to the light, and adds that the Baptist is not the Messiah. I believe that John himself was first of all a disciple of the Baptist, and perhaps initially approached the latter with the secret hope that he had found the Messiah. From Luke 3:15 we know that many people in Palestine wondered if the Baptist was in fact the Messiah. There was obviously an aura of holiness about the Baptist. But the Baptist no doubt explained to John that he was not the light itself, only its witness. In John 1:29 the Baptist talks about Jesus at much greater length than he had talked about himself a few verses before, when priests from Jerusalem asked him to explain who he was. I imagine that the Baptist had a similar pattern of interaction with John. He was reluctant to talk about himself, but eager to speak of the coming Messiah. The Baptist lived in the physical desert, but was also a man of the interior desert, a man of prayer.

He lived simply, eating locusts and wild honey, and dressed himself in camel skin. The Baptist was devoted to God, his spirit was truly alive. He had even begun to proclaim Jesus before his own birth, when he leapt in the womb of his mother (Luke 1:44) in response to Mary's greeting. He was still possessed by the Spirit as an adult. This was why he was pure enough to see the Spirit descending upon Jesus like a dove (John 1:32). And it was the ray of the Spirit that enabled the Baptist to recognize the light that had come into the world. This truth was revealed to the Baptist on account of his holiness, rather than because of his blood kinship with Jesus.

The words uttered by the Baptist in John 1:29 must have stamped themselves indelibly in the mind and heart of John. The Baptist looked at Jesus and called him the Lamb of God who carries the sins of the world. John first gets to know Jesus through the prism of Jesus' own cousin, the Baptist. There was no better spokesman for Jesus available. After all, Jesus himself solemnly says (Matthew 11:11) that of all the children born of women there has never been a greater one than John the Baptist. The testimony of the Baptist would thus be peerless. The great humility of the Baptist is evident in the freedom with which he encourages his own disciples to leave him and turn to Jesus. He does not count this as a loss, but as a gain: "He must become greater, I must become less" (John 3:30). The Baptist, great as he appears in the eyes of the people, knows he is not worthy to untie Jesus' sandals. John learns from the humility of the Baptist. As time passes, John sees a greater richness in this metaphor of the Lamb, first heard from the lips of the Baptist. First of all, it would have reminded any devout Jew of the lamb's blood sprinkled on the doorposts of the

Israelites in Egypt so that when God was striking down the first born of the land, he would "pass over" their Jewish homes and spare their children. It would also bring to mind the story of Abraham and Isaac, when Abraham promised his son that God himself would provide a lamb for the sacrifice on Mount Moriah. And of course it recalled Isaiah's prophecy about the lamb led to the slaughter, who would have no words to say in his defense. In the course of Jesus' ministry, John will be called to imitate the Lamb in carrying sins, specifically the sins of Judas. We will see how John, unlike the other apostles, already carried the sins of Judas long before the betrayal. He knows that Judas is greedy, a thief, and a liar, and these are burdens that he has to carry as part of being a lamb. Let us turn now to the first encounter of John with Jesus.

In John 1:36 the Baptist, with two of his disciples, once again sees Jesus and repeats, "Look, the Lamb of God." One of these disciples is named Andrew. The other is unnamed. I believe that this other disciple is John. The reason I believe this is because such discreet silence about himself is John's signature. This innate reticence is also a manifestation of his humility. When Andrew and John start to follow Jesus, he turns and asks them, "What do you want?" These are the first recorded words of Jesus in John's Gospel. These opening words take the form of a question. And not just any kind of question, but one that is open, free, and intensely personal. It is a liberating question. Jesus could have dictated his own manifesto, he could have issued an ultimatum. But instead, with great humility and profound respect for their freedom, he wants them to discover their own desires. And although they do not realize it, he waits like a beggar, hoping that they will see that it is really him that they are seeking.

Their answer is in the form of a question, "where are you staying?" It seems almost Irish to answer a question with another one! Like God's question to Adam in Genesis, this is not a geographical question but a deeper, more spiritual one. They have just left one master, John the Baptist. They want something lasting now. They want peace for their souls, they want a guide and master in the path of goodness. The Greek verb used in their question is a form of *menein*, which means to lodge, to dwell, stay, remain, be present, endure, abide, last, or live. It is a key word in the Gospel of John, appearing on forty separate occasions. They want to know what he lives for, because that is what they want to live for. They want to know where he stands, because they want to stand with him. They want to know what is the center of his life, because they want to be centered like he is.

Later in the Gospel, when he compares himself to a vine and the disciples to branches, Jesus uses different forms of the verb *menein* over half a dozen times in the space of a few sentences (John 15:4-7). Jesus points out that trying to improve ourselves and be morally perfect are not essential. What is vital is the living connection between the branch and the vine. We do not need to worry about bearing fruit. It is enough to remain with him or abide in him, and he will take care of our fruitfulness. In every grapevine the branches are intimately and inextricably interlinked. The whole plant forms a complex, interlocking organism. Of ourselves, we are helpless. But if we have the humility to acknowledge dependence on God and interdependence upon each other, we can rest assured. To abide is to be in a relationship of love with the Son of God, it is to surrender ourselves to him as Lord of our lives, and to stay united to him and in community with others. The serenity of abiding distinguishes the spirituality of John from the more impassioned and inflamed discourse of Saint Paul. It is an energy that is quieter than the incredible dynamism that animated Paul's missionary travels. Ultimately, John will be called to remain or dwell with Jesus in a contemplative and mystical manner. This is why, in the epilogue to the Gospel, Jesus tells Peter somewhat mysteriously that he wants the beloved disciple to abide until he comes.

But for now, Jesus invites John and Andrew to come and see where he dwells. Many years later, when writing his Gospel, John retains a precise memory of the time of his first meeting with someone who changed his whole life. John notes that it was about the tenth hour, or 4 o'clock in the afternoon. We do not know where they went with Jesus, or what they spoke about. They stayed with him until the following day. Perhaps this is because it was Friday, the eve of Sabbath, and since under Jewish law one could not travel any distance once Sabbath had begun, they were obliged to remain where they were. They had time to speak and to listen to Jesus. Perhaps Jesus told them something of what we read in the Prologue: The fact that he was the light who had come to enlighten every human being, but that he was entering into a world where many were in darkness and so did not understand who he was. But to those who did welcome him, he would give the supreme gift of becoming children of God. In any case, Jesus promises John and Andrew that to stay with him will mean a qualitatively different kind of existence. Saint Augustine once noted the symbolic significance of the fact that the tenth hour at which the two disciples met Jesus corresponds numerically to the number of commandments given by Moses. Their discipleship begins at the tenth hour but goes far beyond it. It is as though Jesus is inviting the disciples beyond a religion based on fear and rules to one inspired by love and the Spirit. I would guess that John had several opportunities to talk with Jesus in the days and weeks that followed, and to speak of what he really wanted, which was simply to love the one his heart had sought for so long. This is what abiding and dwelling concretely meant for him. Having the self-forgetfulness of the humble person, John did not so much want to tell Jesus about himself as to find out all about his new master. Jesus might have told him about Joseph's death and also about his beloved mother whose house he had left to start his life of ministry.

We do not know anything of Judas Iscariot's first meeting with Jesus. We have the barest of information on his background. "Iscariot" refers to the fact that Judas was from the town of Kerioth, some twelve miles south of Hebron. So he was a Judaean, unlike John, who came from Galilee. John mentions that Judas' father was called Simon (John 6:71). But there is no indication at the beginning that Judas is any different from the other apostles, apart from the fact that, writing in retrospect, none of the evangelists can bring themselves to mention Judas Iscariot's name in the list of those chosen by Jesus without also mentioning the unmentionable fact of his awful crime of betrayal. Judas Iscariot's Judaean background may have set him apart from the less sophisticated Galilean disciples. But whatever the cultural differences, Judas Iscariot had something major in common with the others: he too was chosen by Jesus to be one of the apostles (John 6:70). And we also know that there must have been a time when Judas was zealous, generous, and loving. After all, he was sent out along with the other apostles to preach, heal the sick, raise the dead, cleanse lepers, and even cast out demons! (Matthew 10:7-8)

His origins in Kerioth and the name of his father are both indicated in a straightforward manner by John. Initially nothing distinguished Judas from the other eleven apostles. It is telling that even at the Last Supper, when Jesus announced that he was to be betrayed, the apostles, who were deeply upset, did not instinctively ask, "Is it perhaps Judas?" Instead they began to ask Jesus, one after the other, "Surely not I, Lord?" (Matthew 26:22) Ironically, the Iscariot himself joined in on the routine, trying to disguise his impending betrayal by asking with an air of perplexed innocence whether he was the one (Matthew 26:25). The agonized questions of the other disciples were humble and true. They showed that each apostle was above all aware of his own weakness and sinfulness. It is revealing that even at this final climactic moment, Judas did not stand out immediately as a potential traitor. Perhaps the other apostles had their misgivings previously, but Jesus undoubtedly encouraged them to interpret Judas' actions charitably. This would have been a challenge for the apostles. After all, it is relatively easy to be good to somebody of undoubted moral integrity, but it is a trying test of virtue to be good to someone who never ceases to irritate us. Thus from Judas' badness, Jesus was able to bring good: helping the other disciples to grow in patience and love through bearing with the weakest disciple.

At the Last Supper Jesus must have looked sad: shortly afterwards in the garden of Gethsemane he declared that his soul was sorrowful even unto death. Presumably Judas looked tortured himself, though for totally different reasons. The others may have misinterpreted this, thinking that Judas empathized with Jesus. The apostles at the Last Supper teach us that humility is about looking into our own hearts as they did, asking whether or not we are possibly traitors. We also learn from them that it is not easy to see into someone else's heart. Despite the fact that about a year before the Last Supper Jesus had said publicly to the apostles that one of them was a devil (John 6:70), either they could not bring themselves to believe that it was the Iscariot or else they were so humble that Jesus' words compelled them to look uneasily into their own souls.

The evil of Judas is not as transparent as the goodness of John. It is not the kind of dramatic evil we see in Hollywood blockbuster movies. There are certainly occasions in the Gospels when evil is clearly and dramatically evident. There are many cases of demonic possession vividly recounted. People foam at the mouth, mutilate themselves, are deprived of faculties of speech or sight, demonstrate superhuman physical strength, and more. In these cases it seems that demons invade the body of the person and somehow control it as though it were the demons' own body. This is the kind of diabolical possession that is sensationalized in horror films. But what is intriguing about the Gospel of John is that it does not recount a single instance of this kind of possession. Does this mean that there is no demonic activity in John? On the contrary, there is a case of demonic possession in John's Gospel that surpasses in intensity of evil any of the dramatic stories of possession recounted in the other three gospels. John depicts a form of possession that is more chilling than anything depicted before or since: the demon that is Judas (John 6:70).

Chilling because its dire nature is allied to a natural invisibility.

John must have realized there was something particularly special about the mother of Jesus when he saw her prompting the first miracle of Jesus' ministry at a wedding feast. After this miracle at Cana, we learn that Jesus, his mother, his relatives, and some disciples remain (that verb *menein* again) a few days at Capernaum together (John 2:12). Almost three years later, John's Gospel tells us that Jesus gives Mary as a mother to the beloved disciple as he hangs from the cross, and likewise gives her John as a son. Jesus does not force this relationship upon either of them. He simply confirms publicly what has already long been a reality for both of them. From those days at Capernaum, John has begun to look on Mary as his mother. And when Mary looks at John she is gladdened by how much he resembles her son. She sees John's spiritual nobility.

The symbol of John the Evangelist is an eagle. Of all birds the eagle flies highest. Certain scholars see the portrait of the beloved disciple in John's Gospel as an idealized one, as a product of the credulous imagination of the early Church. Perhaps the portrait reflects the truth much more than these sceptical scholars allow. (However, this is not to suggest that John was perfect—we will presently see that his purity and zeal also had a shadow side of intolerance and anger.) Jesus tells us that the pure of heart shall see God. John's purity enables him to soar higher than the other apostles. He eventually rises to a level that is almost angelic in elevation. An eagle is also distinguished by a keen sense of sight. John discerns hidden mysteries with the eyes of the heart. Finally, eagles tend to live to a great age. Again, John "remains" longer than all the other apostles as a contemplative presence in the early church.

Jesus could see into Judas' heart. He saw the little beginnings of Judas' big sin. But he wanted to help this hurting disciple as much as he could. Because of John's shining goodness, Jesus may have sent them together on missionary trips, hoping that some of John's goodness might rub off on Judas. Judas undoubtedly started out well, for at the beginning he left everything to follow Jesus, but he seems to have allowed his heart to become increasingly corrupt.

Judas may have been the most naturally talented disciple. He was pragmatic and efficient, knowing how to deal with money since he had responsibility for the common purse (John 12:6). He was self-confident and assured, mixing easily with the top religious echelons in Jerusalem (Matthew 26:14-15). We have a sense of how deceitful he turned out to be, since he managed to conceal successfully his callous plan for the biggest crime of all. However, he did not become treacherous overnight. After a fervent beginning it was, presumably, a matter of half-lies, guile, and cunning. He saw that deception could open doors and lubricate potentially frictional political scenarios. He may have used his position as treasurer as well as his Temple connections to try to push Jesus as a political and social liberator. He did not want to understand Jesus the way Jesus understood himself, as a Savior of sinners. Sin was something Judas did not really want to free himself from.

Although I have described John in angelic terms, he also had a beastly side. John shared Judas' selfishness, ruthlessness and thirst for power, but was able to channel these feral energies in the direction of service. Here are a couple of instances from the Gospels that throw a less flattering light on John's character: toward the end of Jesus' public ministry, John and his brother James ask the Lord to place them at his right and his left in glory (Mark 10:37). In Matthew's version, their mother pushes them forward brazenly (Matthew 20:20-21). Even the way John and James pose the question is incredibly self-centered. "Teacher," they said, "we want you to do for us whatever *we* ask" (Mark 10:35). Another incident from the end of Jesus' ministry in Galilee demonstrates why Jesus nicknamed John and his brother James "sons of thunder." When the inhabitants of a Samaritan village refuse to offer Jesus and his disciples hospitality, John and James ask the Master if they can use their new-found authority to call down fire upon it (Luke 9:54). There is a precedent for this: the fiery prophet Elijah did the same to the messengers of King Ahaziah of Samaria hundreds of years beforehand. John and James want to do this out of love of Jesus, but their passionate and burning love is clearly sullied by anger and pride. Jesus rebukes them for this manifestation of intolerance. Because John shares qualities with Judas, it makes sense that Jesus might encourage the son of Zebedee to spend time with the Iscariot, in the hope that he might inspire Judas to channel his own formidable energies into service of God and others.

A crucial moment in the metamorphosis of Judas from a generous disciple to a deadly one is the episode in the sixth chapter of John where we are told of the disenchantment of a large number of disciples at Jesus' declaration of himself as the bread of life. Jesus offers the gift of his own flesh and blood to the disciples. Many cannot accept such humility from Jesus. This saying is too hard. A large number of disciples turn away. Judas does not go away physically. Instead, he distances himself in spirit. Without explicitly naming Judas, Jesus announces to the twelve that one of them is a devil. In case we still have any doubt, John adds that Jesus was speaking of Judas Iscariot (John 6:71).

What does it mean to be a devil? We know that the devil is without truth, a liar by nature, and "the father of lies" (John 8:44). We know from the temptation in the desert that the devil tries to entice Jesus to use his power to cure the problem of hunger and to boast that he is the Messiah, before finally tempting Jesus to renounce his power altogether in order to adore Satan himself in exchange for the riches of the whole world.

If Judas is a devil, his character must correspond in a recognizable way to this portrait of the devil. That Judas was a liar is evident from John 12:6, where we also discover that he is a thief and avaricious. But by asserting a correspondence between these other elements in the depiction of Satan and traits of Judas' character, I infer that Judas repeatedly urged Jesus to resort to miracles, to power, to idolatry, not for the sake of the Father, but in order to cut a good figure in front of the people. I believe that Judas wanted Jesus to take a road similar to that taken by Dostoevsky's Grand Inquisitor.

Judas believed that Jesus was good, but misguided, misled by misplaced humility, by excessive goodness, and by otherworldliness, whereas he was the man who knew the world. He believed that Jesus' perfect love, expressed in such extravagant largess as the gift of his flesh and blood, was radically unsuited to an imperfect world. He wanted Jesus to temper honesty with dishonesty, to blend morality with immorality, to add untruth to truth in order to win people over. He wanted Jesus to cultivate the wealthy and influential, to grant himself the luxuries that his status deserved. He thought he would magnify Jesus by doing this, but in fact it would have reduced Jesus. Had Jesus acquiesced, his life would have been centered on something external, something material. Rather than really possessing the world, Jesus would have been possessed by it. Judas wanted Jesus to force people to believe in him, to humiliate those who showed no respect. Judas would agree with Machiavelli that it is safer to be feared than to be loved because of the fickleness, falseness, ingratitude, cowardice, and avarice of human beings. Had Jesus given in to this temptation, he would have eroded human freedom and would have become the object of secret fear and boiling resentment from the very people professing allegiance to him. Judas wanted Jesus to become idolatrous, to feed on the crowd, on their adulation, and on his power over them, instead of feeding upon the will of the Father.

In Chapter 12 of John's Gospel, Judas once again draws our attention, for tragic reasons. He shows his true colors shortly after the final and most extraordinary miracle Jesus works in the Gospel of John—bringing a dead man back to life. We need to appreciate the wonder of this miracle to understand how despicable Judas' behavior was. The raising of Lazarus from the dead was not the first occasion on which Jesus brought someone back to life—he had already done so with Jairus' daughter and the son of the widow of Nain. But they had only been dead for a short time; their bodies had not begun to decay. Lazarus, however, had lain four days in the recess cut into a rock face. It may not seem a long time for us, but for maggots and bacteria it is. The big stone at the entrance would not stop various types of insects from getting into the tomb. Nature has designed them to find bodies as soon as the person expires, and often before, especially when there are open wounds. The linen wrappings would have bought Lazarus some time, but not a lot. Flies would immediately lay eggs on the cloths, and maggots would swarm around, trying to invade where access was easiest: the eyes, ears, nose, and mouth. While maggots were invading Lazarus from outside, bacteria and microorganisms already inside spread throughout his body, devouring it in their quest for the nourishment that they had until then received from Lazarus' daily diet. With speedier decomposition due to the hot climate, the sepulcher was full of a repulsive and putrid odor when Jesus ordered them to remove the large stone that kept it sealed. In case we forget this, Martha clearly says that the corpse of Lazarus already smells, since it has been inside for four days (John 11:39). Jesus remained outside when calling Lazarus to come forth since the odor inside the enclosed space was overpowering.

When the mourners saw the ghostly figure stumble from the cave, there was absolutely no doubt that this man had died, and had been dead for a significant amount of time. Lazarus was called back from the brutish other side of death. Only those who did not *want* to believe could refuse to do so. No doubt many people recoiled at Lazarus' approach, terrified at the sight of this man and frightened of contracting ritual impurity. Jesus told Mary, Martha, and those closest to Lazarus to unbind him and let him go. Now they touched a brother who once again had blood coursing through his veins and a second chance at life. And Lazarus himself, after the initial disorientation, must have felt exhilarated to be alive.

Whenever we get a second chance, it is exhilarating. Judas must have received many chances at life. Jesus per-

haps explained to him that the destiny of the Messiah was
not to be one of power, of triumphing over Rome and over-
throwing the ruling classes. Perhaps Jesus even encouraged
him to reconsider his calling as an apostle: better to be a just
and simple believer than to become an increasingly unjust
apostle.[5] Jesus could read Judas' heart. He could see the
falsehood and the greed. He knew that Judas was not suited
to be a follower of his, because he did not want to be like
Jesus himself.

For his part, Lazarus puts on a sumptuous meal at
Bethany for the One who brought him back from the grave.
While Jesus reclines at table, Lazarus' sister Mary kneels
before him, pours a precious perfume over his feet, then
wipes Jesus' feet with her hair. It is a gesture of utter love,
adoration, and reverence, and a sign of great gratitude for
the life of her brother Lazarus. And perhaps the use of the
expensive perfume is also a sign that she wants to give up
all her wealth and standing in order to follow Jesus in his
poverty.

Mary's gesture of love was the crown of a wonderful
evening for Lazarus. It expressed the deepened love and
veneration that had been awakened in the whole family by
Jesus' staggering miracle. The faith of the disciples was
also strengthened at a crucial time when the gathering oppo-
sition to Jesus from the religious authorities was threatening
to undermine it. As they all beheld Mary at the feet of Jesus,
and inhaled the fragrance that filled the house, their hearts
were uplifted. The aroma of the ointment more than made
up for the stench that had filled the air when Lazarus' tomb
was opened. They could still remember Mary throwing herself at Jesus' feet, tears streaming from her eyes, and her
heart-rending words, "Lord, if you had been here, my broth-

er would not have died" (John 11:32). And now Mary was again at the feet of Jesus, doing what only servants were expected to do. But that is what she wanted to be more than anything else: a faithful servant of Jesus. As she poured out the nard on his feet perhaps a few of those present sensed that she was emptying all of herself along with it, and that she, like the other Mary, Jesus' mother, surpassed the male disciples in her faith and love. A short time later Jesus would wash his own disciples' feet at the Last Supper to show them what love and service were all about. But Mary did not need this lesson. She already gave love in exchange for love. While the majority of those present did not grasp the deeper significance of Mary's gesture, everyone was nevertheless deeply moved—everyone, that is, except for one man: Judas was intent on spoiling the party.

"Why wasn't this perfume sold for 300 denari and the money given to the poor?" (John 12:5) From a monetary point of view, Judas' objection made sense. A denari was equivalent to a day's wage, enough to provide for a family's basic needs. Three hundred denari almost amounted to a year's earnings. It was a considerable sum of money. The nard used by Mary was an especially expensive perfume that had to be imported from India in a sealed alabaster jar. Once the jar was opened, the contents had to be used quickly before they lost their fragrance.

The perfume was certainly exorbitant in price. But Jesus was the Lamb destined for Passover sacrifice, more priceless than any perfume. Mary's gesture was prophetic, not only because she was preparing his body for burial, but also because she was pouring out all she had in anticipation of Jesus' infinite self-emptying.

Judas' objection is completely out of character with this joyous occasion. And it is not just a comment he mutters quietly to one or two people: he proclaims it spitefully before everyone. Even were this objection sincere, and we will see that it was not, no guest says this kind of thing publicly before his hosts, especially in the Middle East, where the etiquette around hospitality is sacrosanct. But the Iscariot had scant respect for Lazarus, being impressed only by his wealth.

John explains to us that Judas complained about Mary's gesture, not because he loved the poor, but because he loved money and stole from the common purse (John 12:6). Because Judas' heart was clouded by evil, he was unable to see the true meaning of Mary's act. And because Mary's heart was filled with love, she saw how important it was to wash Jesus' feet in anticipation. Judas' greed blinded him to her goodness. Since Judas was proud, he did not want to venerate Jesus himself, and could not understand that someone else would express their veneration in such a daring manner. Veneration for Jesus was not in the Iscariot's mind at all. In fact, he had already decided to betray the Master (Matthew 26:14).

How did John know that Judas was a thief? It is unlikely Jesus would have told him. At the Last Supper Jesus only indicated to John that Judas was the traitor in response to a specific question and with the implicit understanding that his answer would not go farther than John. Neither would Judas have told John. I presume that John may once have accidentally come across Judas rifling through the common purse. Jesus knew Judas as he really was. John, following in the way of the Lamb who bore the sins of the world, also found himself carrying the burden of the knowledge of Judas' avarice at this point.

The next decisive moment in the tragedy of Judas is at the Last Supper. Jesus stoops down and washes the feet of each disciple. His overriding concern is to seek out the one who is lost—Judas. Jesus practices what he preaches ("I have not come to call the righteous, but sinners to repentance"—Luke 5:32.) Jesus' perfect love has driven out demons, raised three people from the dead, cleansed lepers, restored sight to the blind, and converted numerous sinners to the path of goodness. If there were still love and goodwill in Judas' heart, his evil would not have been able to withstand Jesus' act of utter humility and devotion. Whatever his sins, whatever his malice, this humble love should have disarmed him. The only reason Judas could successfully resist Jesus' infinite love was because perfect hatred filled his heart. It was not that the Iscariot's hatred weakened Jesus' love in any way; Jesus' love continued to be infinite love. Tragically, the Iscariot remained impervious even to the most exquisite appeal. He had voluntarily given his heart away to hatred. We are told that even before this meal the devil had prompted Judas' heart to betray Jesus (John 13:2). For three years he had witnessed miracles. For three years Jesus' sublime teaching had been proclaimed in his presence. For three years the Iscariot had the benefit of the best spiritual formation from the greatest spiritual guide. But Judas persisted in pride, in not wanting to understand.

After Jesus finished washing the disciples' feet and took his place at table again, he spoke to them about the necessity of serving one another. Then he announced that one of them was about to betray him (John 13:21). Peter asked John, who was next to Jesus, to ask the Master who the traitor was. Jesus tells John that it is the one to whom he is going to give his morsel of food. Judas must be within arm's length of Jesus. If John is on Jesus' right, Judas could very well be on Jesus' left. The position at the host's left was a place of high honor at a meal. Jesus may have invited the Iscariot to this preeminent position to reaffirm his love for Judas and to entreat this wayward disciple to abandon his evil ways.

Jesus does not tell John who the traitor is but explains to him that he will convey it by a sign—sharing his bread with his companion [interestingly this English word comes from the Latin "bread with," *com panis*]. Since Jesus does not say who the betrayer is, the other disciples do not hear a name mentioned. And anyone who notices Jesus giving the piece of bread to Judas presumes that this is a sign of special honor—doubly so, if Judas is sitting immediately to the left of Jesus.

As soon as the Iscariot has taken this piece of food, Satan enters him in an even fuller manner (John 13:27). It must break Jesus' heart to see a man die spiritually before him, though the others, with the exception of John, do not realize the gravity of what is happening: "The biggest danger, that of losing oneself, can pass off in the world as quietly as if it were nothing; every other loss, an arm, a leg, five dollars, a wife, etc. is bound to be noticed."[6]

Jesus gives the Iscariot the cryptic instruction to do what he must do now. Apart from John, the other disciples do not understand the significance of Jesus' words. Since the Iscariot has charge of the common purse they presume Jesus wants him to buy more things for the feast or to give some alms to the poor. What about John? There are abysses opening up within him. His world is collapsing around him.

He has just discovered that Judas is about to betray Jesus but he cannot share this dark secret with anyone. John remains the hot-tempered "son of thunder" as he was christened by Jesus (Mark 3:17) and this fiery side of his character may be fighting to assert itself now. Perhaps he feels the urge to pursue Judas and throttle him. He also feels a deep loneliness and shame—the one he loves most is about to be betrayed and he is helpless to do anything. Jesus is troubled (John 13:21), but this is unlike any sorrow John has ever seen before in the Master's eyes. John does not know how to relieve Jesus this time. None of the usual words seem appropriate. He is on the painful route to wisdom.

John is so disheartened and exhausted that he falls asleep three times, as do Peter and James, in the Garden of Gethsemane. Meanwhile Jesus, like the oil press from which Gethsemane gets its name [Hebrew: *gat shmanim*], is being pressed like olives as he agonizes over his impending passion, one that is going to make him into spiritual nourishment for humankind. When Judas turns up with the cohort of soldiers—a ludicrously large number considering the harmlessness of the one they arrest—John runs away with the rest of the eleven. But a new and stronger John is about to emerge. John soon regains some of his fine heart, because we are told that he ushers Peter into the courtyard of the high priest while Jesus is being interrogated inside (John 18:15).

How could a poor fisherman from Galilee gain access to the residence of the high priest so readily? The truth is that John was not poor—we know that his father employed workers on his boat (Mark 1:20) so the family's fishing trade must have been a profitable concern. In any case, John has ready access to the high priest's dwelling. And he uses this connection in order to help Peter. He senses that it is vital for Peter, the leader of the apostles, to represent the others by being there in solidarity with Jesus. This might give some small crumb of consolation to Jesus.

Meanwhile Judas falls apart. Like Adam and Eve he believed that this sin would make him like a god. He did not simply betray Jesus for the sake of 30 pieces of silver, the equivalent of 30 shekels. That was only a pittance. He did it to make a name for himself, to receive the adulation and praise that he felt was being denied him by following Jesus. But like Adam and Eve after their sin, Judas' eyes are opened. What he sees is terrible—his own spiritual nakedness. Having severed his relationship with God, he is faced with himself—a rotting spiritual corpse. He returns to the Temple and angrily flings the 30 pieces of silver at the high priests (Matthew 27:5). As the hollow sound of the coins echoes on the marble floor, Judas runs away, realizing that divesting himself of the blood money will not rid him of the terrible guilt he feels because of the innocent blood he has betrayed. The blood of the murdered Abel cried to the heavens for his murderous brother Cain; now this new and deadlier Cain is haunted by this blood that would still redeem him but which he continues to resist. Although he is plagued by remorse, he has not yet repented. There is a tree at Golgotha where he could drag himself and find boundless forgiveness. But the Iscariot does not go to the tree of life. He finds a tree of death. It is unutterably sad to see a life of such promise disintegrate into such hopelessness. Perhaps in those final moments, he found a way to humility, to see that God's mercy was even greater than this sin of all sins. Maybe he finally stopped measuring God by his tiny standards. Perhaps he found salvation before the end of the rope found him.

The next time we come across John is near Jesus' mother Mary at the cross. John goes to Mary and tells her what happened as gently and sensitively as he can. He brings her to the place of crucifixion. And as his long-drawn-out agony comes to a close, Jesus entrusts his mother to John and gives her John as a son (John 19: 26-27). It will be some time before John feels the support of her motherly love. First, he will have the delicate and supremely difficult task of trying to console her. She will feel utterly distraught in the hours after Jesus draws his last breath.

I do not believe that Mary was as composed and serene as she is presented by Michelangelo in his *Pietà* in Saint Peter's Basilica. This exquisitely polished marble sculpture depicts Christ on his mother's lap, just after he has been taken down from the Cross. Although it is a supremely beautiful work of art, it is too perfect to be true. The wounds of Jesus are too discreet to be real. It is too far-fetched to believe that Mary could have supported the dead weight of Jesus so gracefully when she herself was weak with grief. Just try holding the weight of an adult body on your lap as Mary is shown doing it in the *Pietà*: you will not feel serene but plainly uncomfortable and distinctly overburdened! This sculpture reflects a dignified and resigned inner beauty that would take Mary much longer to attain. Only at that point would she have adopted the gesture Michelangelo gives her, holding forth the body of Christ to us for our veneration. In the immediate aftermath of Jesus' death, she needed John to hold *her*. When Jesus entrusted his mother to John, no doubt he had a mystical and ecclesiological meaning in mind. But he knew his mother. He knew how much she loved him. He knew how distraught she would be. He knew she would need John in those dark moments. And John was the only apostle who was capable of helping her. John tells us that Mary Magdalene, from whom Jesus had cast out seven demons (Luke 8:2), was the first witness of the Resurrection. She was obviously a woman of extraordinary courage, one of the tiny group who stood by Jesus at the cross. Whatever those seven demons may have been, Mary Magdalene had made heroic progress in the path of discipleship since she received the privilege of setting eyes upon the risen Lord before any of the apostles. Had John been a jealous type, he might have neglected to tell this episode. But he was humble enough to rejoice in the good fortune of others, as though such happiness were his own.

The Gospel that John wrote reveals a man who has gone through awe-inspiring chapters in his own life. They are crystallized in the moment of reclining at the breast of Jesus and discovering the hidden secrets of his love. This great student of love and love's knowledge likes to abide in silence, drawing little attention to himself. But if you read his Gospel carefully you will notice the profundity of John's vision and how down to earth his gaze can be. The prologue to the Gospel is sublimely mystical. But like all true mystics, he notices the details of life, and considers them to be worth recounting: the five porticos at the pool of Bethesda (John 5:2), the six jars of water at the wedding feast of Cana (John 2:6), and even the 153 fish hauled ashore by Peter after the Resurrection (John 21:11). His love makes him light, and after the Resurrection he outruns Peter, reaching the empty tomb before him. Yet he waits for Peter to enter first. He is the pure and humble lamb that is exalted by God,

135

becoming a majestic eagle that soars with wings of love to reach high places. He can help us to fly as well.

It was not only in Jesus' time that apostles fell short of their calling. The stories of priests who have committed unspeakable acts in our own day show that Judas' betrayal was not a one-time event: even today the worst traitors continue to emerge from Jesus' innermost circle. It is possible, like Judas, to be born into a well-adjusted family, to receive a good education, to go to a fine seminary and sit at the feet of the finest teachers, only to turn around and destroy the lives of innocent children. And meanwhile one can preach the redeeming nature of Jesus' death each Sunday from the pulpit, refusing to admit that one's own life is adding horrendously to Christ's agony. It is sobering for us priests to acknowledge that the greatest evil may be perpetrated by those who are offered wonderful opportunities for goodness. The Gospel of John teaches us that membership of the elite circle of Jesus' closest friends only invites holiness; it offers no guarantee of automatic goodness.

John of Zebedee, the Beloved Disciple, ascended towards the light. Judas Iscariot, the Traitor, descended into the darkness. John wanted to love God fully, to give himself completely to God, to lead a virtuous life and control his passions. He listened to the truth that came from Jesus' mouth. He became absorbed into God so that he lived more and more in the light. In God's light he understood the world in a fuller and more perfect way. But it seems that Judas wanted to give himself freely to evil, to lead a bad life. He continued to listen to the lies that the serpent uttered to his spirit. The poison penetrated him and despite the nearness of Jesus, Judas was not cleansed of this poison because he did not want to become clean. As he was drawn into darkness, Judas developed a higher yet warped intelligence, one focused on harming his fellow human beings. And yet to the casual observer, these two men were simply two apostles of Jesus. Evil was not written on Judas' forehead; John did not seem any better than the others.

John and Judas both lived in a time of mercy, for life is always that kind of time. John used his time to make friends with God. He had the wisdom to receive God gladly when he came into his life. Judas was foolish enough to let God go. He became a slave of sin. And all the gold in the world, never mind 30 shekels, would not have been enough to set him free. Perhaps he did turn to Jesus in the last seconds of his life; if so then those chains that bound him were broken.

The intertwining stories of John and Judas demonstrate that the issue of being spiritually alive or spiritually dead is anything but trivial and unimportant. Their stories show us that throughout our lives, we live in a time of choice. And the choice is up to us.

8

Wake Up, Sleeping Beauty!

The world will be saved by beauty.
Fyodor Dostoevsky, *The Idiot*

The fairy tale called "Sleeping Beauty" tells the story of a beautiful princess who is cast into an enchanted sleep for a hundred years, until a prince succeeds in getting through the briar hedge surrounding the castle, breaking the spell with his kiss. This story is curiously reassuring: it lets us know that there is nothing unusual about being asleep; it is part of being human and even happens to princesses. What went on inside the beautiful woman's head for the hundred years she tossed and turned in her sleep? Did she dream? And if so, about what? Did she ever dream of the prince?

God is the prince who sees the royalty inside each one of us. He is the one who surpasses all our expectations and the prince we dreamt of in our deepest selves. He sees our beauty as his sons and daughters. And it is only his love that can break the spell of our enchantment. In the light of his love, we see our own beauty and learn to embrace our humanity. We accept ourselves as we are—creatures and not gods. The original sin of Adam and Eve was a rebellion against creatureliness, and all sins ever since have been crass or subtle variations on this first revolt. As creatures our beauty is not perfect; it is a finite and limited beauty.

My beauty does not originate in me. I am created by God, embedded in a society, generated by a history. I do not exist outside of a world. The bond between the self and the world is more intimate than an umbilical chord: "I" am a relational event. I naturally tend to imagine myself as the center of the world; although on reflection, I come to the ironic discovery that I am alone in doing so! We realize how relational we are when we are reborn through falling in love or are destroyed by love's betrayal.

The reason the sin of Adam and Eve damages them so much is because it damages their relationships. It is not as if there is a sudden transformation in a series of individual substances; it is not as though everything in paradise mutates in unprecedented and terrifying ways. God remains the same. Certainly he upholds the promise he made to Adam that he will die because he has eaten of the fruit. But he nevertheless still shows his love for them by eliminating the serpent on their behalf, by promising that the woman's heel will crush it, and by making clothes for the couple before sending them away from the garden. Adam and Eve are still Adam and Eve. But what alter radically are the relationships Adam and Eve have with God, Creation, and each other. Everything God has created continues to be beautiful and good in itself. All that God has made is good for Adam and Eve, as long as they are in the right relationship with God. But when they turn away from God, everything that was a blessing for them now becomes a curse. When they are in harmony with God, their nakedness, probably a metaphor for their creatureliness, is never a cause of shame.

When they eat the fruit of the tree, they see their humanity as a curse, as something of which they are ashamed before God and before one another. Christian theologians have been tempted in past times to believe that the Fall fully obliterated the image and likeness of God within us, as though we had entirely lost our beauty. Our view of the Fall's effect is not as bleak today. We may be damaged masterpieces, but thanks to Jesus' sacrifice, we can also be restored. It is important to stress our similarity (*not* our equality) to God since so many of our doubts and misgivings conspire to refute it. The mundane upheavals and upsets of everyday life are enough to throw even the best of us off balance. Each of us needs to hear the voice of God, reminding us of his image within us, of our nobility and greatness. Each of us needs to learn and re-learn Jesus' command: "Love your neighbor *as yourself.*" Jesus makes this command so fundamental because he knows how easily we fall into self-hate.

In 1894 the Danish writer Henrik Pontoppidan, later to win the Nobel Prize for Literature, wrote a short story called "Flight of the Eagle" [*Ørneflugt*], which deals with the way our cultural conditioning can inhibit the discovery of our greatness. Given my admiration for the apostle John, it is not surprising that this story attracts me. Pontoppidan tells the tale of an eaglet discovered by some boys and taken to a presbytery, where he is brought up by the pastor and some kind people. He lives happily in the farmyard of the vicarage, surrounded by quacking ducks, cackling hens and bleating sheep. Although this is the only life he knows, he feels an indefinable longing for something more. A few years pass, and one stormy day, as he sits on his usual fence, dreaming sadly of another kind of life, he stretches out his wings in longing and instead of falling to the ground is carried by a gust of wind to the roof of the barn. Never before has he seen the earth from this height. He looks this way and that, until, drawn by the blue heavens and the billowing clouds, he extends his wings again and lets himself be carried upwards, flying uncertainly at first, then more boldly, until with a cry of delight, he arches his streamlined body into a powerful curve, high up in the sky, and finally feels that he is an eagle.

The day declines and he feels nervous as he flies through immense spaces with strange landscapes below. As the sun sets he watches a flock of crows flying home to their snug nests near the houses of human beings. But suddenly he hears a sound and looks upward to see a female eagle circling above against the blazing orange of the evening sky. His sense of bewilderment vanishes and he follows her over the mountains, while the dark forests rustle beneath and the rivers roar through the deep gorges. But eventually he loses heart. He does not want to follow her any more. His wings feel too weak and too heavy. He decides to return to his cozy farmyard. He flies through the night and in the early hours of the morning approaches his beloved childhood home. Tragically, a farmhand who has not heard of the eagle's disappearance mistakes him for a wild eagle, and shoots him dead.[1]

The story of the eagle is unutterably sad. First of all, because it took him so long to take wings and fly away from a culture that stifled his greatness. Think of what he missed all those years: the immensity of the skies, the expansive freedom and joy of flying, the majesty of knowing that he was truly a prince among birds. He actually believed that waddling around a farmyard and pecking at leftovers embodied the summit of happiness. The second reason why this story is heartrending is that when he finally dared to believe the dream, he faltered. He could not cope with his freedom. He could not trust the fact that happiness could be his. And so he happily returned to imprisonment, to wretchedness, to death. John the Divine is the apostle who soared because he did not hesitate fearfully in the face of obstacles, because he did not minutely analyze every difficulty. His eyes were fixed on the Light and he flew directly towards it. He was truly an eagle.

The reality of our daily lives continually confronts us with evidence of our fragility and brokenness. This woundedness is part of who we are. But the very fact that we are not satisfied with this sorry state of affairs is already a sign that we have a sense, however inchoate and undefined, that we are also made for so much more.[2] If we were only quacking ducks and cackling hens, we would be content with our mediocre lot, for we could never have known better. But since we are called to greatness, it is not surprising that this voice makes us restless with longing. We do not want to graze all our lives in the anonymous pastures of bovine mediocrity. Not only do we have the dim collective memory of descent from a royal couple exiled from Eden; we also have the pledge of an even more lofty inheritance because of the life and death of Christ. Through him we can call ourselves sons and daughters of the Most High. The one we dare to call Father has fashioned a vast and dynamic universe where new galaxies explode into birth billions of light years away, while the delicate webs of microcosmic life spin at dizzying speeds, invisible to our naked eye. And finding ourselves somewhere between these extremes of enormity and minuteness, we straddle both. In the film

Casablanca, Rick says to Ilsa, "It doesn't take much to see that the problems of three little people don't amount to a hill of beans in this crazy world." But because of the Christ-event, our little problems and everyday concerns add up to more than a Mount Everest of beans. They are the problems and concerns of a royal people. God looks at us and does not only see sinners; he also sees his sons and daughters. I wish we could do the same.

Our eagerness to take flight as eagles is evident in the great desires we all harbor. Hundreds of years ago the great Italian mystic Catherine of Siena told us that we have nothing infinite except the soul's love and desire. But few of us cherish the grandeur of these desires. They are the only infinite things about us, the only ways in which we "touch" God, so to speak. Everything else about us is finite and limited. But all frontiers are powerless to hold back the infinite longing that wells inside. The Danish thinker Søren Kierkegaard was so disillusioned with the absence of passion in his contemporaries that he used to return to the plays of Shakespeare, for there at least he found people who were human beings in the most expansive sense of the word, people who loved and hated, who forgave and cursed, and who differed so refreshingly from the shopkeeping souls who surrounded him in the suffocatingly provincial surroundings of nineteenth century Copenhagen. The Irish poet William Butler Yeats lambasted the stingy materialism of his contemporaries who had let a nobler Ireland die while all they did was "fumble in a greasy till / And add the half pence to the pence" (*September 1913*).

Thankfully, the experience of love can often awaken the sense of our own beauty. We all long for nourishing variations of that magic phrase, "I love you." We trust these words. We trust that somehow these words are all that really need to be said. They encompass and transform so much: our desires, our dignity, our doubts, our disillusionments. They pour all these qualities into a vast and unlimited ocean. Like Hamlet, none of us escapes "the slings and arrows of outrageous fortune." Yet it is vital that these arrows do not darken the skies so much that we no longer see our nobility. A genuinely humble man never forgets that he is a prince; a fully alive woman knows herself to be a princess.

We live in a world where crooked lines cannot always be straightened. We cannot disentangle doubts from faith because the doubts of our world wound the faith of each of us. We are weighed down by the burden of unbelief, and not primarily religious unbelief, though that as well. First is the lack of faith in ourselves. It would be reassuring if we could sort it all out more easily. In a world of instant communications, we expect split-second solutions. It would be tempting to abandon mystery and embrace magic, to shift from process to snap. The wiser route is patience with our own hesitancies. If we rush ahead we risk undermining our vacillating sense of self-acceptance. The epic drama of our lives cannot be shrunk into Instamatic resolution, however much we want a happy ever after. We are pilgrims on an ambivalent journey, seeking to become real and at the same time thwarting it, yearning to live and veering towards self-destruction, longing for innocence and plaguing ourselves with guilt. We never know the privilege of linear lines and straightforward progressions. Our lives take zigzag routes, with unexpected loops and detours.

To be humble is to know that one is an eagle with clipped wings. No wonder we fear flying. The invitation is not to lose our trust and to focus our threatened energies on love. If we manage to respond to that difficult double call, we will perfume the earth with a fragrance that lingers. It is not a matter of telling ourselves how great we are, pushing positive thoughts, propping up our self-esteem with Prozac. It means being graced with the realization of our immense value through friendships, through prayer, and through the myriad ways God colors the tapestry of our everyday lives.

Being earthen vessels, we labor to carry our treasures to others. But sadness and joy go hand in hand. To be humble is to cultivate the asceticism of being joyful, to risk the ups and downs of life rather than to slam down the shutters and hide our vulnerability. This joy does not flow without effort: it swims bravely against the currents of unhappiness in our lives. When someone advised the poet Rilke to undergo psychotherapy, he is said to have responded, "If I lose my demons I am afraid that my angels will take flight as well." I am not sure what he meant by that response, but it is true that we all live with weaknesses as well as strengths. I like to imagine that he preferred the struggle of sharing his gifts while not shying away from his weaknesses. Life with either greatness or wretchedness might be more straightforward, but it would certainly be less human. We are not called to deafen ourselves to who we are, shuffling through muffled lives in a monophonic world. Instead we are invited to join a chorus that sings Hallelujah in glorious stereophonic sound.

Our service of other people is aided immeasurably if we can see their beauty. Such perception smoothes the path to service; loving them even becomes a joy. According to Hans Urs von Balthasar, if beauty is discarded, then the appeal of goodness is diminished:

"If the *bonum* lacks that *voluptas* which for Augustine is the mark of its beauty, then the relationship to the good remains both utilitarian and hedonistic: in this case the good will involve merely the satisfaction of a need by means of some value or object, whether it is founded objectively on the thing itself giving satisfaction or subjectively on the person seeking it."[3]

Of course beauty and goodness are not identical. Beauty and goodness may certainly complement each other, but obviously the goodness of something requires much more than it simply being attractive. Beauty is essentially satisfying symmetry, perfect proportion, and sublime simplicity. Such exquisiteness is bound to attract us. The good also attracts us and this is one of the reasons that it is easy to confuse beauty and goodness. In Dostoevsky's *The Idiot*, Nastasya Filippovna embodies precisely this ambiguity of beauty. Against her own advice, Prince Myshkin naïvely identifies her beauty with goodness. When Prince Myshkin turns up uninvited at Nastasya Filippovna's birthday party she asks him: "'So you think me perfection, do you?' 'Yes.' 'You may be an expert at guessing, but this time you're wrong.'"[4]

We can see the inner beauty of others if we can see the presence of Jesus in them. The beauty of Jesus ultimately resides in the striking harmony we find between his finite human nature and the infinite divine nature revealed through it. This beauty is not accessible to the dispassionate spectator or the scientific observer. It presupposes receptivity and the capacity to allow myself to be taken up into a dynamic movement that carries me toward him. And when he draws me to himself, he inevitably draws me to others. He gives my life a new plot, one centered on service.

Because Jesus' beauty is most of all revealed in the moment of his greatest humiliation upon the cross, I am invited to see his beauty most of all in the poor and disenfranchised. John the Evangelist does not give an account of the Transfiguration in his Gospel because for him the whole story of Jesus' life and death is the unfolding of a transfiguring tale, one that finds its moment of greatest beauty in the instant of deepest humiliation—the crucifixion. Before his death Jesus had promised: "But I, when I am lifted up from the earth, will draw all men to myself" (John 12:32). To be raised on the cross is the glory of divine beauty because it is the greatest manifestation of God's love. And this love attracts: "I will draw all men to myself."

Humility is cheerless misery unless we have a sense of our own beauty, itself a gift from God, and unless we know the encouragement of being drawn by divine beauty. Humility begs for the affirmation that reality is ultimately good, that it radiates splendor, and that the power of God irrigates our deserts with clear and flowing waters. God wakes us up and shows us our attractiveness and that of others. He does not want us to remain sleeping beauties. A strong sense of our beauty helps us live with our big responsibilities. And we have some big ones, as we will learn from exploring Fyodor Dostoevsky's *The Brothers Karamazov*.

9

Responsibility for All

And that we are all responsible all for all, apart from our own sins, you were quite right in thinking that . . . And in very truth, so soon as human beings understand that, the kingdom of heaven will be for them not a dream, but a living reality.
Fyodor Dostoevsky, *The Brothers Karamazov*

If we are half-awake or intermittently comatose, then we are only really aware of a fraction of the wonder of life. We become so inured to our comatose culture that when other people wake up spiritually, the semi-aware begin to wonder if they are the ones with the brain injuries. We ask, "What has gotten into him?" or exclaim "She has really gone crazy this time!" If I live only for myself, I misunderstand the real point of life. This means that I will be bewildered by some-one who lives their life for others. I will see their wisdom as foolishness. If I only truly trust what I see—money, people, a top job in my company—then it will seem madness to trust unconditionally in God, who is invisible to my eyes. If I believe that I am only responsible for myself, then I will be aghast at the suggestion that I could be even remotely responsible for everyone else. Yet the truth is that we are all in this together, we are all responsible one for the other.

Here I want to turn to the great fiction of the Russian sage and novelist Fyodor Dosotoevsky, where we find eloquent testimony to the effects our individual lives can have on the lives of others. Dostoevsky calls us to responsibility for all. First, let me begin with two powerful impressions of Russia that have struck me through cinema and television.

I saw the film *Doctor Zhivago* for the first time recently and was struck by the sheer size of Russia and the mammoth scale of its history. During this epic movie, there is an almost endless train ride from Moscow to the Urals, through a vast and beautiful landscape. There is Yuri's painful trek through unimaginably lonely steppes. There is the sense of countless human tragedies that surface briefly only to be swallowed up again.

Although historical details are somewhat tangential to the love story at the heart of the film, it conveys some rudimentary sense of the enormous upheavals Russia experienced in the early twentieth century. The character of Lara, played by the beautiful Julie Christie, seems like a metaphor for Russia. Three different types of men want this long-suffering woman—Yuri, the soulful romantic; Komarovsky, the scheming capitalist; and Strelnikov, the cold and idealistic Communist. After she has been violated by Komarovsky, while troops brutally repress a student demonstration in the street outside, the connection between her suffering and that of her country is captured by a shot of the bloodstained snow of mother Russia.

I still have a vivid memory of an episode of a superb British documentary series, *The World at War*. To the accompaniment of the unforgettable voice of Sir Laurence

Olivier, it showed the long and bloody German invasion of Russia in World War II. Despite the initial success of the ruthless Operation Barbarossa launched on June 22, 1941— by the beginning of December German troops were on the outskirts of Moscow—it inevitably crumbled in the face of the seemingly limitless Russian resources of men and materials, the implacably bitter Russian winter that froze weapons and tank fuel, and the enormity of a country that stretched infinitely in all directions. Without signposts or milestones, the Germans often felt they were making no progress. There was a particularly memorable scene of the December 1941 Soviet counterattack: exhausted German soldiers stared in disbelief as hundreds of fresh Siberian troops in camouflaged white outfits with machine guns slung across their shoulders suddenly appeared from nowhere, rapidly skiing towards them across the eerie white landscape.

Fyodor Dostoevsky showed how vast the interior landscape of the human soul is.[1] He himself suffered. As a teenager he lost his mother to illness while his father was murdered, apparently by the serfs on his own estate. During four years of labor camp imprisonment in Western Siberia he encountered the spectrum of human life, especially criminals who lived at an intensity and pitch rarely witnessed in the comfort of polite society. Perhaps this is why his novels are peopled with characters who seem too extravagant to be real, human beings who can commit cruel murders only to dissolve into tears over minor upsets, men and women who get carried away by mystical transports and are still heartless enough to trample over other people.

During those years in Siberia he had the opportunity to read and re-read the Bible, and there is a rich biblical undercurrent in his writings.[2] It is as though his works evoke the beginning of everything in the Book of Genesis, exhaling the prime and unformed energy of creation. Dostoevsky's extraordinary creativity did not come cheaply. Towards the end of his traumatic years of imprisonment he contracted a severe form of epilepsy, from which he was to suffer for the rest of his life. He was repeatedly on the brink of financial ruin.

Given his turbulent life, it is not surprising that Dostoevsky's novels dramatically combine the vices of murderers with the virtues of saints, at times in the same character. This is especially evident in *The Brothers Karamazov*, completed by Dostoevsky only two months before his death, and thus a last testament of sorts. The same blood that urges the brothers toward life and goodness impels them toward vice and depravity. The father Fyodor Pavlovich, although vulgar and heartless, is also touchingly innocent. He plays the idiot, mocks spiritual people, and deeply respects his religiously inclined son Alyosha. He spouts out conversational garbage with ease and in the midst of ludicrous digressions delivers scathing insights. He is the careless father of four sons, one of them, Smerdyakov, the fruit of the heartless seduction of a simple woman who lived in the village. Smerdyakov, although despised by the family, with the exception of Alyosha, turns out to surpass even his mentor Ivan in cleverness, and claims to the latter that he has murdered their father at Ivan's behest. This is a deep shock to Ivan, who has been unaware of his tremendous impact on his half-brother. Ivan is the cold intellectual who also cares passionately about innocent suffering and for this reason rejects God. He succumbs to an illness that damages his reason and seems the ultimate consequence of his intellectual pride. Dmitri, the eldest brother, although spontaneous and generous, can also descend to moments of mindless savagery and although he does not kill his father, he accepts punishment for this crime. Fyodor's youngest son Alyosha, the protagonist of the novel, is morally admirable and wishes to become a monk. But he too has to struggle inside himself with the darker impulses that are common to all the Karamazovs in their thirst for life.

There is an emphasis on the power of humility in *The Brothers Karamazov*. The spiritual father of Alyosha, the saintly elder [*staretz*] Zosima, teaches that "Loving humility is marvelously strong, the strongest of all things and there is nothing else like it."[3] The most fascinating influence behind this teaching on humility is the Gospel of the Beloved Disciple. Yes, John, the pure and humble disciple, continues to bear lasting fruit—on this occasion in one of the most gripping novels of all time. John's influence is hinted at from the beginning. The epigraph of the novel is taken from John 12:24: "I tell you the truth, unless a kernel of wheat falls to the ground and dies, it remains only a single seed. But if it dies, it produces many seeds." This Johannine verse must have meant a lot to a man like Dostoevsky who had received a last minute reprieve from execution at the hands of a firing squad and who was then thrown like a useless grain of wheat into the frozen ground of a labor camp in Omsk. This biblical verse is also a profoundly autobiographical comment on Jesus' part. It sums up his life—and his death. Jesus speaks these words shortly after Mary has anointed him at Bethany, and immediately after his triumphal entry to Jerusalem. The crowds are ecstatic at his arrival; many of them instinctively see this unlikely Messiah on a donkey as their political liberator from Roman rule. Jesus declares to his disciples that the hour has come for the Son of Man to be glorified (John 12:23). I am sure they liked the apparent triumphalism of these words: "*Now* he's talking!" But the solemn declaration about the grain of wheat must have sounded totally askance, a complete *non sequitur* to the promise of glory that went before. What is glorious about falling to the ground and dying? Wouldn't it be much more glorious to be crowned a king and to receive the adulation of the whole of Israel? Judas, who had not been at all excited by Jesus' "bread of life" discourse in John 6, must have looked patronizingly on the One born in Bethlehem (literally "house of bread"), who was going on about one of his obsessions again—bread, this time by way of wheat. In fact Jesus was talking about many things, above all about how he, a solitary grain when his passion begins, would produce a whole loaf of bread—an enormous batch of believers— through his death. And in this way he would bear real fruit to counteract the rotten fruit that Adam and Eve ate in the Garden of Eden. In this verse from John's Gospel, Jesus was comparing his death to sowing, which to all appearances destroys the grain, but in reality helps it multiply by breaking through the hard outer husk in order to free the life inside. It is not about death for the sake of death. It is death in the service of life.

Of course it demands humility to deign to fall into the dirty, cold clay and a reservoir of hope to trust that the damp coldness will not submerge us in the end. The elder Zosima lives out this humility in an early scene that brings together for the first time the principal characters of the novel. This uncomfortable meeting for all concerned takes place in his monastery, which Alyosha has just entered as a novice. The immediate reason for this extraordinary family gathering is Fyodor Pavlovich's desire to settle the protracted and vexed question of family inheritance and the valuation of their estate with his estranged son Dmitri, in the presence of witnesses. The bone of contention between father and son is in fact their common love for Grushenka, a woman of doubtful morals and definite allure. Dmitri is late in arriving, a delay which provides his father with the opportunity of playing the clown, firing a barrage of questions at the elder Zosima, with all sort of unexpected biblical citations included, with the unintentional consequence of proving that even someone quite devilish can quote scripture. In response Zosima urges Fyodor Pavlovich to attack the root of his problems—self-deception. Fyodor Pavlovich has lied so much to himself that he is no longer sure what is true and what is false in himself or others, and so he has lost all self-respect and disrespects others too. He gets offended easily, and derives a perverse pleasure from feeling insulted, often inflating trivial criticisms for sheer pleasure, all the while allowing hatred to ferment within. Fyodor Pavlovich has built such a palace of illusions around himself that he no longer knows where his real self dwells. He thus lacks accurate self-knowledge, an indispensable ingredient of true humility. In a surprisingly lucid moment regarding himself, Fyodor Pavlovich concurs with the elder's analysis, practically quoting John 8:44, and acknowledging himself to be a liar and the father of lies.

When Dmitri eventually arrives, an acrimonious family discussion erupts as charge and counter-charge are hurled across the room, before Zosima, instinctively sensing the subterranean violence that is ready to explode at any minute, takes action. Dmitri, coldly furious at his father, has

155

just growled "Why is such a man alive?" His father responds, "Listen, listen, monks, to the parricide."[4] As a fight threatens to break out, Zosima, with great effort, lifts his frail and sickly frame from his seat, and, with the assistance of Alyosha, moves toward Dmitri. Zosima bows before Dmitri until his forehead touches the ground and pleads, "Forgive me, all of you!" This gesture of the Elder entails becoming a subject in the sense of "*sub-jectum*," freely taking upon oneself the weight of the world. In this gripping scene, where Dmitri rages ferociously against his father and Zosima echoes Jesus' washing of his disciples' feet, the polar oppositions of the novel are prefigured and symbolically enacted: murderous hatred and life-giving humility.

The whole theme of guilt [*vinovat*] or responsibility is of capital importance in this novel. Ralph Matlaw, who revised the classical Constance Garnett translation, notes in his afterword, "On Translating *The Brothers Karamazov*,"[5] that our responsibility for everyone and for everything is the principal idea of the novel, and that the word "guilt," one of the most crucial words in the novel—he does not even mention the more pointed and controversial term "sin"—can lead to difficulties:

> The crucial cluster is the word "guilt" along with its derivatives and attendant ideas. In the legal sense, guilt and sentencing and judgment are clear, at least linguistically. But ethically and morally their implication differs. Since the leading idea of the novel is that "we are all responsible for everyone and for everything," it would not have done to translate the word "responsible" as "guilty," for that would both

limit the meaning and introduce an unwarranted legal note, perhaps also a more specifically psychiatric connotation than Dostoevsky may have intended. Indeed, the same word "guilty" (*vinovat*) colloquially and most frequently means "excuse me" in Russian or, to get a closer shade of meaning, "pardon me." Dostoevsky studiously avoids this usage throughout the novel.[6]

Essential to humility in *The Brothers Karamazov* then is the deeply-held conviction of one's own responsibility, a responsibility that surpasses that of anybody else.[7] The first occasion on which these startling words about responsibility are uttered is when the saintly monk Zosima becomes weaker and draws towards death. This episode is reminiscent of the farewell discourse of Jesus in the upper room in John's Gospel, chapters 13 through 17. Only the disciples hear Jesus recapitulate his message of love. In a similar way, Zosima desires to share what is most precious to him with his monks, all the things he wanted to say during his life but had never managed to express. And the wisdom that is dearest to the elder Zosima turns out to be the insight into one's own responsibility for everyone. It is only when this responsibility is acknowledged and appropriated by the monk that he truly reaches the summit of his vocation. Paradoxically, this enormous sense of responsibility does not lead to bitterness, but softens the heart.[8]

Zosima first learns this lesson in humility from seeing a grain of wheat fall into the ground and experiencing its fruitfulness in his life. The grain of wheat in question is his brother Markel. The falling into the ground is his brother's terminal illness. The fruitfulness is the spiritual transformation that accompanies it. This conversion is expressed in his brother's extraordinary newfound happiness allied to a profound sense of his own unworthiness. The power of Markel's conversion is summed up above all in his enigmatic and momentous claim: "Every one of us has sinned against all men, and I more than any."[9] His mother, puzzled by these words, gently remonstrates with him. Perhaps these words sound dry and juridical to her. But for Markel these words represent a consoling and heartfelt knowledge. He once again insists: "Believe me, everyone is really responsible to all men for all men and for everything."[10] This awareness of his limitless responsibility coexists with a burgeoning love for humankind and all creation, and is suffused with a boundless sense of gratitude. The impact of Markel's words does not register with his mother and family. Although she had prayed for his conversion, she had perhaps expected some more confined and comprehensible transformation in her son. Even the local doctor finds the young man's declarations so bizarre that he concludes that the disease must be affecting Markel's brain!

It is only much later, after his brother's death, that these words begin to bear fruit. They mark Zosima's life in an indelible manner. The words of Markel touch Zosima so much that they help effect his conversion from a nominal belief to a personal and all-consuming faith. Zosima has just deliberately and publicly insulted a rich landowner who married the girl he wanted for himself; as a result they arrange to engage in a duel the following morning. Zosima returns home that evening and takes out his fury on his batman. Zosima beats him to the point that the servant's face is covered with blood. The next morning Zosima wakes up and the scene re-enacts itself in his mind: his own ferocious cruelty and the utter lack of resistance proffered by his servant. He realizes all of a sudden that this servant is a fellow human being of equal worth to himself. He bursts into tears and at that moment the words of his deceased brother insinuate themselves into his consciousness. Zosima wonders to himself: "In truth, perhaps, I am more than all responsible for all, a greater sinner than all men in the world."[11]

Zosima realizes also that he is ready to kill another man in a duel, a man who had never wronged him, and thus deprive the man of his life and the man's wife of her happiness. Zosima first of all drops at the feet of his batman, bows his head to the ground, and asks for forgiveness. By his words and action he thus reverses the "master-slave" relation of before. His servant, still rigidly entrenched in a hierarchical framework, is convinced that his master has become a stark raving lunatic! Zosima then goes to the place of the duel and, after his opponent has taken the first shot, he flings his own pistol into the trees nearby. Then he turns to his adversary and pleads for forgiveness, declaring that he, Zosima, is at least ten times worse than him.

Zosima's fellow officers find his views so original and unworldly that they take to calling him a monk. They find his talk of vicarious and universal responsibility to be worthy of a reaction that veers from polite amusement to outright ridicule. A mysterious stranger begins to visit him and points out that it takes humility to ask for forgiveness, and to be willing to take the consequences of being regarded as a simple-minded fool. This appropriation of everyone's guilt is not the kind of integrity that has much currency in society. In fact, it seems ludicrous. Yet the stranger is convinced that were this stance to be understood and adopted by all, the kingdom of heaven would become a reality upon the earth: "And in very truth, so soon as men understand that, the Kingdom of Heaven will be for them not a dream, but a living reality."[12]

After Zosima's death, his humble teaching percolates through to various characters. Again the grain of wheat is at work, bearing fruit for a multitude, even for people who never personally met the *staretz*. In his final discourses, Zosima had encouraged his monks to irrigate the earth with their tears, happy tears of compassion, like the joyous weeping that accompanied the final days of his brother Markel. Alyosha and above all Dmitri are set awash with tears that increasingly soften their hearts.[13] Dmitri, for instance, wrongfully charged with the murder of his father, begins to feels that he shares in the guilt. Even the strong-willed Grushenka, initially cast as a femme fatale, comes to feel guilty for the way she has damaged the relationship between Fyodor Karamazov and Dmitri.

But isn't this vicarious responsibility over the top? Isn't Zosima taking humility too far? A person is usually only held responsible for their own actions and omissions, or if they are accomplices in another's crimes, or are negligent in informing someone of their duties and obligations. But in *The Brothers Karamazov*, responsibility extends to everything that happens and to everything done by others. The origins of this excessive responsibility are not simply in Orthodox spirituality, but in the Bible. The Jewish prophets were known to do crazy things, like Hosea who married a prostitute in a living echo of God's stubborn faithfulness to his people, despite their infidelity. Jesus was dismissed as a fool, dressed up as a mock king, and then crucified. Saint Paul went to the crazy lengths of rejoicing in the "madness" of the Christian message. However, the tradition of being a fool for Christ's sake (1 Corinthians 4:10) has historically found a warmer welcome in Eastern Christianity than in the West, despite the fact that the most popular Western saint is undoubtedly the one who most shows this exuberant abandon—Saint Francis of Assisi. But in the West holy folly tends to be tolerated as an exception to the rule, whereas in the East the divine eccentricity of the holy fool[14] is revered as an elevated form of sanctity.

I find that this teaching on responsibility makes sense in my own life. I know that as a follower of Christ, I have not done all I could to serve others. Too often, I have opted for the comfortable option instead of the right way, for the avenue of least resistance instead of the path of greatest generosity. Rather than standing for God, I have fallen for everything else. Instead of focusing on the most important things in life, I get bogged down in the most urgent. I have deprived my brothers and sisters of the love I owe them. Markel's life and words had a profound effect on his younger brother Zosima, whose example and teaching in turn touched the lives of many people in Dostoevsky's novel. Were I a better person, there would be more saints around today as well. If I loved more, fewer people would turn to evil. I have not come anywhere near to loving God with all my heart, and all my strength, and all my soul, not to mention loving my neighbor as myself. I have sinned through omission, through failing to do so much good.

Those who have true faith are deeply compassionate like Zosima. If others are ungrateful or indifferent, they do not judge them but try to love in their place. They implore God for their conversion in the name of all that Jesus suffered. In the name of the Son they ask the Father to shower his love upon young and old, black and white, women and men, rich and poor. And their trust of God is so enormous and bold that they continually expect he will do the extraordinary. They try to tell everyone of God's love, but most of all they incarnate this love in their own lives, for they know that the purpose of life is to be consumed by love. And they realize too that most people are bad because nobody has loved them enough. Neither do these compassionate people rely on their own resources. They unite themselves in spirit with all who love God, have loved him, and will love him. They trust that God will answer them because of his infinite love, not because of any right they have. They know how to make a creative link between their own littleness and God's greatness. They truly believe that they are worse sinners than anyone else alive. Yet they do not let their own vulnerability frighten them, since they draw continually on the immensity of God. Indeed they realize it is their very littleness which draws God's mercy towards them—after all, he converted the world through a dozen apostles. They never want to escape his presence. They know they are speaking to God when they talk with their neighbor. And they lend their own voice to God so that he may speak through them. When their words touch hearts, they know that it is not because of them, but because of the heart of God which has touched others through them. They live so focused on God that their hearts resemble the Garden of Eden before the Fall, a space where God can walk freely and speak to them at any time. They do not live in a comatose culture but in the very heart of God—this happy and constant unfolding of infinite love.

I certainly need to rediscover the humility of Zosima and Francis of Assisi. There is something deeply attractive about these men—their goodness radiates. The example of the saints is also sobering—it makes me realize how proud I am. Indeed I am so far from the holy folly of the great Orthodox pilgrim saints that I even get annoyed if someone calls me a fool! But more than merely revealing my inadequacy, the stories of the saints invite me to change my life. The beauty of their goodness is a summons to conversion. These giants of Russian spirituality and literature woke up from their comas. May their tears of compassion bear fruit for the Russia of this new millennium.

10

Living Humility with Hope
in Holy Week

But ours is the long day's journey of the Saturday.
Between suffering, aloneness, unutterable waste on
the one hand and the dream of liberation, of rebirth
on the other.

George Steiner, *Real Presences*

Apocalyptic theories have gained great currency of late,[1]
especially in the wake of the terrorist attacks of September
11, 2001. The Coalition War with Iraq has done little to alle-
viate these end-of-the-world feelings. Although those who
won the war are actively trying to win the peace, there is a
fear of further conflicts and of new recruits to terrorism.
Some regard a rift between Islam and the West as the defining division of this new century. Others turn their attention
to the increasing evidence of global warming. They fear that
climatic changes may bring disastrous consequences for our
planet.

When we turn to the Bible, we certainly come across
general information on the end times, but little of a specific
nature: there are no dates given for the end of the world, no

particular human being is identified as the Anti-Christ, and so on. Shortly before his Passion, the disciples asked Jesus how they would know of his return and of the end of the world. Although he indicated some signs that would indicate that the end was near, he also made it clear that his return would be as unexpected as the flood in Noah's time, or as a burglar stealing into a house in the dead of night. Regarding the exact moment, Jesus declared: "No one knows about that day or hour, not even the angels in heaven, nor the Son, but only the Father" (Matthew 24:36). Can we then speak of an impending Last Judgment? We can say that the end is near once we are clear that "near" does not mean the same thing to God as it does to human beings: "With the Lord a day is like a thousand years, and a thousand years are like a day. The Lord is not slow in keeping his promise, as some understand slowness" (2 Peter 3: 8-9). For God time is even more relative than it was for Einstein.

A healthy dose of humility enables us to see that the Bible's references to the end times are not intended to fuel idle curiosity, but instead to encourage each one of us to conversion. We will have little interest in converting if we feel we have no need to. And the horror of apocalyptic wickedness conjured up by our imagination practically absolves us of our own petty sins by contrast. With such dramatic scenarios engaging our minds, it is tempting to forget that there is at least a little badness even in the best of us. We can forget our guilt and ignore our own failings while we gloat over evil elsewhere. We can get much more than a sliver of *schadenfreude* from imagining the comeuppance that *really* bad people will get in the final cosmic showdown. Their deserved demise contributes to the delight of speculating about the strange happenings associ-

ated with the end of the world. For instance, people identify the harlot of Babylon in the Apocalypse with everything
from Western civilization to the Catholic Church to the
Jerusalem of the future. They breathe a sigh of relief, "thank
God I am not with any of *them*!" But as we learn from the
episode of the adulterous woman in the eighth chapter of
John's Gospel, only the one without sin has the right to cast
the first stone. We would be wiser to look into our own
hearts: perhaps Babylon is us, all of us. We have all fallen
short of true goodness. In this third millennium we cannot
exactly boast that we have made a roaring success of our
own lives and our world. It is quite possible that God has
made other worlds, with creatures who have lived the life of
love much more fully than we have. Although talk of UFO
sightings is probably always a question of wishful thinking,
it does not surprise me that if (and it is a very big "if") we
have been visited by aliens in flying saucers, we only have
fuzzy and blurred photographs to show for it. No doubt they
decided to speed away as fast as possible when they saw the
mess we had made down here. On an even more whimsical
note I enjoyed coming across the following zany lines from
Douglas Adams' *The Hitchhiker's Guide to the Galaxy*:

> On the planet Earth, man had always assumed that
> he was more intelligent than dolphins because he
> had achieved so much—the wheel, New York, wars
> and so on—while all the dolphins had ever done was
> muck about in the water having a good time. But
> conversely, the dolphins had always believed that
> they were far more intelligent than man—for pre-
> cisely the same reasons.'[2]

Whatever the imminence of the Second Coming, I believe that in these early years of the twenty-first century we find ourselves in a period like Holy Week, the name given by the Church to the liturgical week that annually precedes the great celebration of the Resurrection. Holy Week is a period in which the last days of Christ's life are commemorated in a special way. I began this chapter with a poignant Holy Saturday quotation from George Steiner. Perhaps Steiner was inspired by Hans Urs von Balthasar, who offers a daring vision of universal salvation in his theology of Holy Saturday.[3] But we have yet to arrive at this Saturday of which Steiner speaks. Certainly there are signs of Holy Saturday in our culture, but they are intimations of something still in the future rather than indications of what is already present. We are situated a little earlier in that final week of Jesus' life, and we do not know how long our own Holy Week will last. Our Holy Week is a confusing time of enlightenment and darkness about our future. We can ignore or get indignant at this dizzying abyss, or we can allow it to become a wake-up call and a stepping stone to new life by uniting our experience with Christ's Holy Week. If we welcome Jesus into our fragile present he will transform this time into one of hopeful humility; he will suffuse our sleepy selves with the energy and life of the Resurrection. In the first chapter of this book, we looked at how worms generate fertility in the soil and make our world a happier and healthier place in which to live. In an analogical way, "digging" into the mystery of Holy Week, when evil was in the ascendancy and goodness was increasingly forlorn and abandoned, can also yield unsuspected riches for our individual and communal lives. However, we need to dig hopefully.

Let me say clearly that the last thing I want is to condone despair about our future: that should never be an approved word in the vocabulary of any Christian. It was only over the gates of hell that Dante put the words, "Abandon hope all ye who enter here." This world should always be a world of hope. It is never wise simply to postpone hope until the afterlife because "the new heavens and the new earth" (Isaiah 65:17, 66:22; 2 Peter 3:13) of which Scripture speaks also find a partial realization in our world. The last things [*ta eschata*—the Greek from which "eschatology" comes] do not only arrive at the end; they also unfold in the here-and-now. Death, judgement, heaven, and hell do not merely belong to the future; it is through the choices that people make in the present that they are already in the process of deciding their final destiny. But above all when one reflects on these four last things, it is imperative to remember that God "wants all men to be saved and to come to a knowledge of the truth" (1 Timothy 2:4). A Christian's hope for the world should mirror God's wish for all of us by being unconditional and unlimited. This hope is anchored in the Resurrection of Jesus. Because Jesus has already risen from the dead, the New Age of which he spoke is partially present now. This New Age is about renewed human beings and a transformed world where justice and peace find a home. This New Age entails a new heaven because heaven is no longer divorced from our present world; it involves a new earth because hope is no longer infinitely deferred to life after death.

If we turn to John's Gospel, we find that Holy Week begins at Bethany, with Mary's anointing of Jesus "six days before the Passover" (John 12:1). In this week before Jesus' death, the disciples were full of unreal hope. They had not read the signs properly. At the beginning of the week they shared the inebriated enthusiasm of the crowds, who hailed Jesus as a king when he triumphantly entered Jerusalem, seeing in him the hope of liberation from Roman rule. Of course the disciples had failed to see the import of his arrival on a donkey (see John 12:16)—a sign that humility and meekness rather than power and brute force were to be the distinctive characteristics of his kingship. All through the week they were still intoxicated by the hosannas of the crowds echoing in their ears. They failed to see that their Master was about to die. When Jesus washed their feet, Peter was taken aback. He did not understand the significance of this gesture. Later in Gethsemane, Peter, James, and John fell asleep instead of keeping awake with their Lord. When Jesus was arrested, the apostles who had left everything to follow him ran away like frightened sheep.

Good Friday opened up an abyss for the disciples, one that continued to fracture their lives on Holy Saturday. They were confronted with their own cowardice. Peter wept bitterly because of his denial of the Master, finding it hard to forgive himself. There was anger at Judas, then shock at the news of his death, and despondency that one of their own could have betrayed the Lord. The death of Jesus had a devastating effect on them all. John and Mary Magdalene hardly had time to think about it. Drained from standing at the Cross, they then did their best to support Jesus' mother Mary in her grief. Easter Sunday was actually only two days away. Despite this chronological proximity, the disciples descended into a chasm reverberating with questions, assailing them with doubts, haunting them with uncertainties, defiling them with guilt, and overwhelming them with gloom. In existential terms, the Resurrection must have seemed light years away for some, an impossibility for others. There was truly a horrible hiatus between death and new life. But this pattern is not limited to that day two thousand years ago. It is an archetypal pattern, one repeated in different guises even in our own time. Emmanuel Levinas' thought, for instance, evokes Holy Week. By saying this, I am not trying to patronize this Jewish thinker by assimilating him into a Christian framework. Rather I am thinking of how his very survival of the Shoah left him in a time that was out of joint, a time *like* Holy Week. Looking back, he saw the deaths of millions of Jews. Anyone who has witnessed the massacre of innocent people instinctively feels guilty for surviving. Living each day with the painful memory of the annihilation of his people, Levinas henceforth found purpose only in a freedom that knew itself to be culpable. When he looked to the future, Levinas was not sure of any great Resurrection of love, but he did trust in the small goodness between one person and another.[4] Caught between the fearful memory of the death of millions and the privilege of its postponement in his own case, Levinas felt that each moment was a Last Judgment, an opportunity to serve one's fellow human being.

The worst day of Holy Week, where suffering was most intense, was Good Friday. The other days were more removed from the immediate pain. There was room to hope and also space to fabricate illusions. From time immemorial millions of people have been experiencing Good Friday itself—the countless people murdered in violence and war, the enormous numbers who have died through famine, perished in natural disasters, or simply breathed their last in desperation, unknown and unloved. But this is not to imply that the rest of Holy Week is painless by comparison. In fact, Holy Week is a curious mixture of exaltation and desolation. There are those who are excited at the prospect of the Messianic future promised by greater wealth, universal peace and a new world order. Meanwhile there are the Holy Saturday people—the widows, orphans and strangers, and all the millions of lives those three categories of marginalized people stand for—surviving but barely living as they are hit almost daily with pain and loss.

What is new is that this Holy Week experience of illusory joy and real grief is now hitting the West too, not just in isolated cases, but in a more continual and all-encompassing way. Some obvious examples are the tremendous benefits promised by new technologies, allied with the profound fears of their unlimited application; the delight of a new post-Communist world order giving way to apprehension at the rise of more diffuse and evasive global terrorist networks. Beneath the thin surface of optimism about a better quality of life, the earth seems to be rebelling against our imperialism—"hell hath no fury like Mother Earth scorned." The bizarre weather, the dramatic floods, the unexpected earthquakes—all these and more may reflect an awakening of the natural world at the very time we are falling asleep and forgetting that we were asked to be its stewards, not its despots.

Today there is a sense of uncertainty infecting people's spirits. And this Holy Week syndrome, although experienced at a deep level, is not always something we can pin down and does not capture the public spotlight so readily. It is like Kierkegaard's harrowing statement, quoted earlier, about the uncanny silence with which a soul can die. It is as though we are vaguely aware that as a culture and as individuals we are falling into a deathly sleep, a spiritual coma, analogous to the sleep that weighed down Peter, James, and John in the Garden of Gethsemane the night before Jesus was crucified. We are like sleepers bereft of inspiring dreams. There are many reasons for this comatose state. As fewer people seek meaning in religion, politics, and class, they come to expect romantic love to offer *the* path to self-realization. Despite the wonder of those we love, they cannot sustain the weight of our exaggerated expectations. We are wounded in our relationships, marriages break up, people who once could not stop saying "I love you" now cannot bear the sight of one another. They fight over a share of their child's heart, and the child tries so hard to give fairly to each that it is afterwards reluctant to give to anyone else. Adults fail in love, then find the new person they hope will be "it"; meanwhile the children pick up the emotional tab. Many children do not even know their fathers today. Innocent children are abused. Unborn children, the humblest and most innocent creatures of all, are denied the right to life. Men have lost their self-esteem along with their jobs. Single mothers struggle to bring up children as normally as they can, in anonymous concrete blocks of flats next to derelict shopping centers full of disgruntled teenagers and volatile drug addicts. Asylum seekers crawl out of trucks or swim ashore from cramped boats and are imprisoned in overflowing detention centers, giving birth to children who do not belong anywhere.

And although the neon signs and television screens never go out, the spiritual guides in our culture are no longer as full of light as they once were: many of them seem beset by more than their own share of shadows and doubts. Tragically there may be some John the Evangelists and

Mother Teresas of Calcutta among those unborn children whose lives were cut short too soon, potential saints who could have helped us reach Easter Sunday sooner. We are weighed down with so much emotional baggage that we are in danger of succumbing to spiritual heart attacks during this long Holy Week. But it is easy not to notice all this and to forget how much our souls miss God. Our culture of spectacle bombards us with such an endless succession of artificial lights that the memory of the true Light falls into forgetfulness.

Our culture desperately needs to hope. To hope is to refuse to be incarcerated in the present. To hope is to strain towards the future even when we seem irremediably leashed to the brute reality of the here and now. To hope is to unlock the doors of our prison so that we might be free. But given the anxiety and distress that weighs our culture down, any hope that rests on weak foundations will disappoint. The more grim things become, the more our hope must be founded on the infinite resources of God. We need to experience God's love for us in all our brokenness; we need to see our immense potential for good reflected in his loving eyes. His love can make Holy Week a hope-filled Holy time, where a fire is kindled despite the gathering twilight, and the flame becomes so luminous that the darkness of destiny cannot overwhelm it.

I do not know what our future will be like. But I do wonder what we would do and how we would behave if we no longer had the social supports and infrastructures that we so much take for granted. How would the devastation of ecosystems or economies affect our behavior? With heavily polluted air, deforested continents, and oceans emptied of living creatures, we would certainly live more impoverished lives at a biological level. Will global climatic changes bring us suffocating summers and Arctic winters? Will our economies collapse under the weight of greed? Will large-scale wars multiply? We hope not. But if they do, how will we take it?

Near the beginning of Douglas Coupland's novel *Girlfriend in a Coma*,[5] Karen, a seventeen-year-old high school student from Vancouver, falls into a coma after consuming a large quantity of vodka and Valium. Shortly beforehand she writes a note to her boyfriend and reveals an indefinable anxiety: "I'm writing this note because I'm scared. It's corny. I'm stupid. I feel like sleeping for a thousand years—that way I'll never have to be around for this weird future." Karen wakes up a full seventeen years later, just before the world ends—sort of—in a single afternoon. Everyone except for her and her six closest friends simply falls asleep. But this worldwide coma does not wake up the tiny group of survivors. The seven survivors of the end of the world initially react with stupefaction, but the shelf life of their shock turns out to be shorter than milk. They soon subside into whimsical apathy. Having failed to read the signs of the times written in capitals all around them, they take to a pattern of drifting rather than decision, of casual destructiveness instead of arduous creation. For the next year they vegetate, watch videos, drink too much, loot liquor stores, and smash up cars. It takes mighty persuasion on the part of the ghost Jared, a former high school friend, to convince them to do something with their lives. I think each of us can be just as deaf and indifferent after the novelty and shock of a crisis wears off.

If our world does change in a dramatic way, will we be even able to face the fact? It is never easy to accept huge change as Wolfgang Becker's playfully serious film *Good Bye Lenin!* (2003) shows. In this film a committed East German Communist, Christiane, has a heart attack when she sees her son Alex being arrested at an animated demonstration against the Party in 1989 when the German Democratic Republic celebrates its 40th anniversary. Little does she know that the days of the regime are numbered. Christiane falls into a coma. When she revives eight months later, East Germany no longer exists. Aware that any excitement could trigger another heart attack, Alex conceals the truth about the reunified Germany from his mother. Although Alex and his sister Ariane have thrown out all the old furniture and fittings, they now recreate their mother's bedroom in all its dilapidated splendor of eight months before. Alex even persuades his friend and colleague Denis, an aspiring filmmaker, to create and anchor a daily television news bulletin for the sake of his mother, one that celebrates the dubious virtues of the now defunct East German Republic.

Although Alex's mother has undergone a real coma, Alex himself suffers from a figurative one. He has refused to accept that life has changed irrevocably. Not that he retains any nostalgia for East Germany; on the contrary, he is more than glad to see the back of it. But he refuses the challenge of growing up and clings to childhood by creating an idyllic East Germany that he knows never existed. Alex's character is especially appealing because there is something of him in each of us. When we look around our world today, we do not want to countenance the possibility that, as William Butler Yeats put it, "a terrible beauty is born." We do not want to see that in our new world order, where Communism has so dramatically collapsed, there are new

176

divisions rapidly rising in its place. We do not want to admit to the cracks and fissures that also threaten to topple the Western world from within. Our noble ideals have not led to the kind of societies they so richly promised. But however comatose we may feel and however sleepy our cultures may become, there is always one jewel that will keep us awake: love. Isabel Allende's bestseller *Paula*,[6] is a poignant and uplifting book about her own daughter's coma and the power of love to outlast even the terrible coma of death and separation. This stirring book shows a way to bridge the divide between Good Friday and the Sunday of Resurrection. It is an autobiographical text that begins with Isabel's vigil at Paula's bedside in a Madrid hospital. It is intended as an extended letter, telling Paula the story of the family, in an effort to give her memories for her awakening, memories that her mother feels are slipping away during the coma: "Listen, Paula. I am going to tell you a story, so that when you wake up you will not feel so lost." Isabel believes that the act of writing will help her give form to the form-less chaos she feels inside, helping both Paula and herself in the process. Isabel has never shared her past with anyone before, but now, fearing that Paula has been dispossessed of her own history, she shares this innermost recess, hoping the memories will revivify her daughter. This harrowing yearlong coma is a drawn out Holy Week of passion, in every sense of the word, for Isabel. Within a month of the onset of Paula's coma, Isabel already feels a century older. Both she and Paula have "entered a zone of inky darkness." She cannot help wondering whether there isn't some lesson that Paula wants to teach those she loves through this coma. Isabel cannot imagine how to console Paula's new and devoted husband Ernesto, since she herself feels so hopeless. Much of the time the waiting is interminable and monotonous, spiced by Isabel's recollections of her own dramatic life and the political upheavals of Chile. There are moments of drama in Paula's coma: she is touched by death when her blood pressure plummets to zero and the monitors sound alarms. Isabel silently begs her daughter to fight and orders her "heart to keep on beating in the name of Ernesto and the precious years you had still to live and for the good you had yet to give." Isabel bargains with God, offering her own life in exchange for Paula's, all the while aware that this cannot cancel the unique destiny each one of us is called to live.

After almost five months, Isabel convinces the doctors and Ernesto to allow her to fly Paula to San Francisco, where Isabel believes the possibility of recovery is greater. But despite a month in a rehabilitation clinic, Paula shows no signs of improvement; on the contrary, only a steady deterioration of her condition is expected. Now that conventional medicine has proved of such little value, Isabel cares for Paula at home, turning for help to hypnotists, psychics, and other unorthodox practitioners. Isabel's mother arrives to visit her granddaughter and is shocked at the sight of her. Ernesto comes to visit and finally admits to himself that there will be no miraculous reunion with his wife. Shortly before Paula passes away, she appears to her mother in a dream, walking gracefully into the room as she did before her illness. Because her mother has not accepted that Paula will never be as she was before, her daughter is unable to cross the threshold of death. She needs her mother's consent to make this decisive step. Although many of her memories have vanished, she assures her mother that she will always carry the memory of those she loved with her as she sets out upon the luminous path that stretches before her. Isabel's brother Juan, a priest, comes to stay for a time, and spends long hours in prayer at Paula's side. He realizes that Paula has swept away the trivialities of their lives and left them only with the essential. She is an angel who has opened the gates of paradise for them and has blessed them with a glimpse of the immeasurable mystery of God. A year after she falls into the coma, Paula passes away gently and quietly in her mother's arms. "I had lost everything, and my daughter was leaving me, but the one essential thing remained: love. In the end, all I have left is the love I give her." The family and friends gathered around Paula experience a mysterious sense of unity following her death, as though her spirit had conjoined them all into a single being. As the book ends, Isabel dreams that she herself is dissolving into a void where there is warm light allied with deep darkness. She feels that she is both herself and also her daughter, that she is nothing and everything. In the midst of the emptiness she senses a meaning that lies beyond her grasp.

Christian faith reminds us that love is eternal. It assures us that darkness will never extinguish the light, even if the light at times seems to comprise no more than a few candles. Although Hegel once described modernity as Good Friday minus Easter Sunday, the darkness of the world is by no means that absolute or unrelieved. The light can never be quenched, as the prologue to John's Gospel tells us with eloquent simplicity. And worry about the future only serves darkness. In fact worry is one of the worst spiritual epidemics that grips the Western world. It is as though we constantly wait for some new sickness, catastrophe, or act of terrorism to worry about. Worry undermines hope, a central virtue for Christians. The more we worry the less we hope in God's loving care and providence. We are invited to believe the heartening words of God from Isaiah 54:10: "Though the mountains be shaken and the hills be removed, yet my unfailing love for you will not be shaken." The more we let things get us down, the less we accept that love is bigger than any of these calamities, however destructive they may seem. If we do not want the catastrophes to throw us off balance we need to develop the capacity to hope and to trust in the midst of the bothers of everyday life. If we learn to live without worry in our daily lives, we will develop the habit of hope, and will be ready for the big shocks which are much less frequent though much more intense. As a rule, we are not challenged to make extraordinary acts of virtue every day. I am not called every day to rescue somebody from a burning building or to jump into the sea to save someone drowning. But someday my time to hope against hope will arrive; now I need to acquire the steady habit of hoping and trusting to carry me through the big test ahead.

If I had to pinpoint the day in which Christianity finds itself in Holy Week, I would guess that it is Holy Thursday. (Of course, this is not to deny that the Church constantly nourishes itself from the death and resurrection of Jesus, so that Good Friday and Easter Sunday are a constant presence.) That was the day when one of Jesus' own inner circle, Judas of Iscariot, betrayed his Lord. The new millennium began in a Judas-like way, especially for the Catholic Church. Once again the most serious betrayers were the ones ostensibly closest to Jesus, just like Judas. Allegations of abuse on the part of pedophile priests that had surfaced over a number of years erupted into a scandal of global dimensions. What was new this time was that there was evidence of cover-ups, as well as the shifting of known offenders from one parish or diocese to another. The people who betrayed children and betrayed God were those with the special calling of apostles. The worst enemies of the Church were its own ministers. Tragically there is always a Judas in the inner circle of Jesus. But it is heartening to remember that there is always someone with the goodness of John among the apostles in a time of crisis as well. I do not know how long this Holy Thursday will last. I do not know whether there will be more betrayals and what forms they might take. But I do know that there will always be men and women of the caliber of John. God will always raise up good people in our midst. We will survive the difficult times.

What can Christians learn from Jesus' humility during Holy Week? Obviously much more than I could ever understand or describe. But let me say something about the humble gesture that began that final and holiest of weeks: entering Jerusalem upon a donkey. It has a lot to teach us. Anyone with an eye to public relations would have suggested that Jesus enter Jerusalem in an imposing chariot, riding a bejewelled camel or a gleaming white stallion. Instead he chose a common beast of burden to arrive through the Eastern Gate from Bethphage. This choice was intended to convey simplicity and humility as the prophet Zechariah indicated hundreds of years earlier: "Rejoice greatly, O Daughter of Zion! Shout, Daughter of Jerusalem! See, your king comes to you, righteous and having salvation, gentle and riding on a donkey" (Zechariah 9:9).

A donkey is patient, constant in purpose, capable of hard and sustained work, and peaceful by nature. What can the donkey teach us about Holy Week? First of all, the necessity of having a contemplative disposition during this time in history. The donkey remained silent and centered amid all the commotion surrounding Jesus. The donkey teaches us the urgency of contemplation, which is to live in the presence of love even without the comfort of light, even without the consolation of understanding. The donkey did not know where this journey with Jesus would lead, but this uncertainty did not cause the donkey to give up. Neither was it distracted by the noise of the crowds. But its contemplation was not ethereal: the donkey was not floating in a fuzzy cocoon. It was concretely connected to the figure of Christ.

Secondly, the donkey teaches us the importance of unhurried work and simple service that are directed to God. This "Holy Week" time is a period when we can get distracted by drama and sidetracked by spectacle and forget that the wonder of salvation unfolds when we plod quietly in the direction that God has set before us through the commandments. The donkey was an animal that worked, not a creature of leisure. Of course, there was no acclaim for the donkey—the adulation was all centered on Jesus. But the example of the donkey shows us that God values honest and constant labor. In fact, the journey Jesus began on the donkey that day was to fulfill the demanding work of loving us by dying upon the Cross. Our work most truly enhances our dignity when it is united with Christ, when it is "God-bearing," like that of the donkey. We are graced with the privilege of creating along with the Creator, of helping to bring the marvel of creation to its realization.

So much for the humble donkey and its profound teaching. Let us now turn to the world of art, to see what we can learn about Holy Week from a painting that gripped Fyodor Dostoevsky. When he was traveling through Europe with his wife Anna Grigorevna in 1867, they stopped at Basle to see a painting that he had heard about. It was Hans Holbein the Younger's stark *The Body of the Dead Christ in the Tomb*, a rectangular life-size oil on wood painting from 1521, which shows the corpse of Jesus lying face up, apparently in a state of rigor mortis, marked with many wounds from his passion and crucifixion. It is said that Holbein used a corpse fished from the Rhine as a model. Whatever the truth of that story, the painting is characterized by Holbein's attention to detail,[7] with clearly green and gangrenous wounds showing evidence of the swelling and decay associated with decomposition.

Holbein's canvas struck Dostoevsky in a forceful way because it did not have the serenity and beauty which painters typically bring to the figure of the dead Christ. Dostoevsky thought it was the kind of picture that could destroy someone's faith. This painting finds its way into his novel *The Idiot*, where the dying Ippolit Terentyev, a highly intelligent young man who sees his advancing consumption as a reason to rebel against God, describes the frightening impact a reproduction of this picture has upon him. He sees this representation of the tortured corpse of Jesus as an obstacle to faith in the Resurrection, as evidence that the devouring and dismembering of death are simply insurmountable: "The compulsion would be to think that if death was so dreadful, and nature's laws so powerful, how could they possibly be overcome?"[8] This interpretation of Holbein's painting has had an enormous impact on how it has been seen subsequently.

But some recent scholarly opinion tends to diverge from Dostoevsky, and to interpret this harrowing portrayal of the dead Jesus as a stimulus to faith, as an invitation to see the Resurrection for the extraordinary miracle that it is.[9] There is no denying the fact that Holbein's painting is stark. It challenges us to have a robust faith. It shows the utter abandonment and solitude of Jesus. There is nothing beautiful about the corpse we see. And yet, as we saw in the last chapter, glory can also radiate where there is surface ugliness. A painting like this can deepen our faith.

Holbein's picture can act as a spur to our faith if we remember that it does not portray the literal truth, but tries to express an insight into the seriousness of death and the wonder of Resurrection. Why doesn't it depict the truth of the events as they happened? First of all, even though Jesus' body was hurriedly prepared for burial because of the proximity of the Sabbath, it was nevertheless bound in linen cloth with spices by Joseph of Arimathea and Nicodemus (John 19:40), whereas in Holbein's picture, Jesus' body is not wrapped at all. Secondly, Jesus' followers would not have neglected fundamental decencies such as lowering the Master's eyelids and closing his mouth, although in Holbein's version both eyes and mouth are wide open. Thirdly, Holbein's painting depicts Jesus as utterly alone: forlorn and forsaken, he still undergoes suffering despite the fact that he has already passed away. But there were a few friends faithful enough to stay by his side, and the intense love of his mother reached him across the murky veil of death.

The truth about Jesus' condition after death is perhaps somewhere between Michelangelo's *Pietà* and Holbein's *The Body of the Dead Christ in the Tomb*. Jesus was neither eloquently serene nor thoroughly forsaken. And the compassion of Mary and the courage of Joseph and Nicodemus have a lot to teach us about how to respond to the pain of others. We have no right to stand by and watch when we encounter the victims of suffering. I am free to accept hardship in my own case and to try and wrest meaning from it. But when it comes to others I am challenged to use my freedom to illuminate the darkness of their Good Fridays.

If the Church is in Holy Week then it will go through some sort of crucifixion experience. This will be extremely painful. Like the apostle Peter, who was scandalized when Jesus predicted his own suffering and death, it is tempting to dismiss talk of an impending crucifixion. It would be humanly more flattering (and spiritually more warped!) to believe that the future greatness of the Church lies in honor and esteem, rather than sacrifice. After all, who wants to lose the respect of the people? Who wants to be lowered to the level of a common criminal as Jesus was?

The Holbein painting reassures me about a vital dimension of the Holy Week of the Church and of our culture. It relieves me with the knowledge that Jesus has already been there, has undergone it before us. He has suffered, died, and descended into the earth like a grain of wheat. It is authentic humility to enter into the *humus* in such a voluntary and surrendering fashion. Jesus has gone further than we ever could in the mystery of Holy Week. He has gone further than you have—if you are reading this book you are still alive. He has gone further than those who have died, not only because of the perfect love and utter compassion with which he fell into the earth, but also because this movement denied in a definitive way the downward gravity of death and instead surged up into resurrection. With Jesus death and descent into the earth were by no means the last word. With Jesus the impossible became possible and death lost its sting. Jesus rose again!

Even in its darkest hours, therefore, Holy Week can be a time of great hope. As the sun rose on Holy Saturday almost two thousand years ago, I imagine that the Virgin Mary had recovered from her immediate distress, had regained her composure. She saw, as faith can see, that the seal on the tomb was not definitive, not the ultimate stamp on Jesus' life, but that it would soon dissolve, giving way to a never-ending story. If we can see Holy Thursday, Good Friday, and Holy Saturday for what they are, we will necessarily see beyond them to Sunday and will not fall into the danger of entombing faith in the folds of forgetfulness. Instead, Holy Week will grace us with the opportunity to live in a spiritually more elevated manner in the midst of our lowliness and dependence.

Now we arrive at the end of our journey together. We have seen that humility is expansive, embracing our relationship with God, with others, and with the cosmos. Humility is helpful both on a personal and cultural level. On a personal level humility is something vibrantly alive, like a fragrant perfume that embellishes our whole Christian life. It enables us to recognize that none of us comes first, that at our core something greater than ourselves is at work. On a cultural level an essential part of humility is to recognize that we have become comatose in a spiritual sense; our era is a Holy Week time, where uncertainty, unease, and illusions are mixed up with moments of truth. However, humility does not keep us from hope, precisely because Jesus' own Holy Week experience led to the glory of the Resurrection.

Humility and wakefulness are vital for our future. Whether or not we are in Holy Week, all of us find ourselves in situations of being stuck, of feeling that we have reached a no man's land. When a relationship breaks up we feel deeply hurt inside. We wake up at night with a stain the size of Alaska on our back. We look backwards only to see emotional debris strewn across the path of our lives. We look ahead and it seems that love has no tomorrow. We have seen how Jesus was betrayed by someone close to him, how he was abandoned by everyone, except for a few courageous woman and one man called John. After an ignominious death, he descended into the cold anonymity of the earth. The consolation I draw from this journey of Jesus is that there are no depths to which we can go that are beyond the loving reach of his compassion. We need never be afraid of sinking into an irreversible coma.

Humility is as silent as Jesus' tomb on Holy Saturday. To speak of it is to be embroiled in the paradox of trying to reveal that which conceals itself, of attempting to give a face to that which is essentially self-effacing. The tomb of Jesus was not an end in itself, but a transition time on the way to the Resurrection. Discussing the "what" of humble wakefulness in this book is also not the ultimate goal of our journey together. Clarifying the "what" is only for the sake of living the "how" more fully. By throwing light on the meaning of humility, the virtue of humility will hopefully illuminate our lives from within. We understand it in order to live it. Humility—which teaches us to rely simply and trustingly upon God rather than on our own resources—will get us through the uncharted terrain of Holy Week, because with God at our side we have already arrived at the Promised Land of the Resurrection.

Epilogue

When you are in a deep coma, you need a good doctor. For this spiritual coma in which we find ourselves, a doctor of the spirit is necessary. Thérèse of Lisieux (1873-1897), declared a Doctor of the Roman Catholic Church on October 19, 1997, the centenary year of her death, is the ideal choice. Not only is this extraordinary French saint universally recognized; she also combines her medicine of the spirit with a strong nursing instinct, for she promised to spend her heaven doing good upon earth. She might be the youngest doctor ever proclaimed by the Church, but she is also one of the ablest.

Thérèse realized that God's love reaches down to our littleness and raises us up to greatness. When we are in a spiritual coma, we have fallen to a real low in our lives. But admitting that we are in a coma need not be a confession of despair, but rather a reason to rejoice. Ironically, the weaker we are, the less strength we feel, the more nothingness we experience, the readier we are to receive Jesus into our lives. But it is essential that we follow Thérèse's prescription and not simply wallow in our own weakness. We need to add limitless trust in God to our sense of smallness. This boundless and immense confidence in God's goodness is the most vital medicine of all.

Thérèse clung to this unbounded trust even when she experienced in an agonizing manner what it was like to live in a world without God. In the tiny confines of her Carmelite convent in Normandy, she was drawn against herself into the worldwide crisis of atheism. Although as a child she always had the certainty that she would one day live joyfully in God's presence, things changed in the last couple of years of her brief life. She felt a thickening fog all around her. It enveloped her more and more, penetrating the core of her being, so that she was no longer able to make out the image of her true country, as she liked to call heaven. Thérèse realized that God had led her into this dark night of the soul so that she might share in the experience of unbelievers. Although she still had the gift of faith, she found it almost impossible to believe in an afterlife. But although her heartfelt certainty of heaven slipped away from her grasp as the icy claws of spiritual death threatened to freeze her very soul, Thérèse refused to abandon her childlike and unconditional trust, thus showing that her way of spiritual childhood was the truest form of heroism.

So deep was her darkness that she realized she would have killed herself were it not for the gift of faith. Her faith meant above all that she never ceased hoping against hope in God's love. Her faith found concrete expression in her prayer, which she famously described as "a surge of the heart, a simple look toward heaven, a cry of recognition and love that embraces both trial and joy."

If anyone's example can help us to live through a spiritual coma and emerge at the other side with even greater confidence and love, it is the example offered by Thérèse. She did not rely on her own powers, but cast herself confidently into the arms of her heavenly Father. She was completely at ease with her own littleness. Even though she knew she would never learn to love properly by herself, this did not discourage her in the least: her focus was not on herself at all. Because she fixed her heart on God's infinite mercy and love, she knew that nothing would be impossible to her. She wanted to be a priest, an apostle, a martyr—in short, she did not want to choose one ministry but all. And through God's mercy she found a way of achieving the impossible, by choosing the central and overarching vocation that embraces every particular Christian vocation: the vocation of love. By loving she knew she could share in the ministries of young and old, black and white, rich and poor, healthy and sick, whether priests, prophets, patriarchs, apostles, martyrs, missionaries, married couples, or singles. She was a woman of astonishing ambition who was content with nothing less than an epic life, yet had the genius to find it in the ordinary. For these reasons and more, Saint Thérèse of the Child Jesus and of the Holy Face (to give this Carmelite nun her full religious name) is the ideal patroness and advocate of the spiritually comatose.

Notes

INTRODUCTION

1. A similar idea is propounded by Marie-Dominique Philippe in *Les Trois Sagesses* (Librairie Arthème Fayard, 1994), p. 356.

ONE: GLIMPSES OF HUMILITY

1. In the words of Phillips: "Darwin, in other words, leaves us with a bafflingly simple question the resonance of which he characteristically understates: What would our lives be like if we took earthworms seriously, took the ground under our feet rather than the skies high above our heads, as the place to look, as well, eventually, as the place to be?" Adam Phillips, *Darwin's Worms* (London: Faber and Faber, 1999) pp. 60-1.

2. Emmanuel Levinas, *Of God Who Comes to Mind*, translated by Bettina Bergo (Stanford: Stanford University Press, 1998) p. 171.

3. With the backup of an enormous amount of empirical research and statistical data, Putnam argues that since 1965 there has been a decline of participation in community activities with an associated deterioration of what he terms "social capital," which he describes as the links between persons and social entities and the rhythms of mutuality and trust to which they give rise. Robert D. Putnam, *Bowling Alone: The Collapse and Revival of American Community* (New York: Simon and Schuster, 2000) p. 19. Putnam sums up his argument as follows: "For the first two-thirds of the twentieth century a powerful tide bore Americans into ever deeper engagement in the life of their communities, but a few decades ago—silently, without warning—that tide reversed and we were overtaken by a treacherous rip current. Without at first noticing, we have been pulled apart from one another and from our communities over the last third of the century." (p. 27).

4. Although not denying the numerous positive aspects of contemporary society, Myers also notes that they co-exist alongside many undeniably negative facts: "Had you fallen asleep in 1960 and awakened in the 1990s, would you—overwhelmed by all the good tidings— Feel pleased at the cultural shift? Since 1960, as we will see,

The divorce rate has doubled.

The teen suicide rate has tripled.

The recorded violent crime rate has quadrupled.

The prison population has quintupled.

The percent of babies born to unmarried parents has (excuse the pun) sextupled.

Cohabitation (a predictor of future divorce) has increased sevenfold.

Depression has soared—to ten times the pre-World War II level, by one estimate.

The National Commission on Civic Renewal combined social trends such as these in creating its 1998 'Index of National Civic Health'—which has plunged southward since 1960. Bertrand Russell once said that the mark of a civilized human is the capacity to read a column of numbers and weep. Can we weep for all the crushed lives behind these numbers?" David G. Myers, *The American Paradox: Spiritual Hunger in an Age of Plenty* (New Haven and London: Yale University Press, 2000) pp. 5-6.

5. See Robert E. Lane, *The Loss of Happiness in Market Democracies* (New Haven and London: Yale University Press) 2000. Lane demonstrates that although economic growth initially increases the level of happiness, subsequently the law of diminishing marginal returns sets in. According to Lane, once the poverty level is surpassed, increased wealth adds nothing to happiness. In fact, as wealth increases it undermines the very sources of happiness—relationships with families and friends—by consuming our available energy and time. Lane recommends willingly forgoing increased income in order to give more energy to relationships.

6. This insight corresponds with the recommendations made by Lane in his study on happiness in developed nations. He believes that supportive relationships, a decent job, and good education are vital to personal well-being. See *ibid.*, p. 335. Lane's recommendations are wise but cautious.

7. Moderate responsibility, let alone excessive responsibility, can be difficult to accept in Western culture. In this regard, Robert Bellah and his co-authors in *Habits of the Heart: Individualism and Commitment in American Life*, (Berkeley: University of California Press, 1985), p. 304, give the following revealing transcript of an interview with a female therapist in the USA:

"Q: So what are you responsible for?

A: I'm responsible for my acts and for what I do.

Q: Does that mean you're responsible for others too?

A: No.

Q: Are you your sister's keeper?

A: No.

Q: Are you your brother's keeper?

A: No.

Q: Are you responsible for your husband?

A: I'm not. He makes his own decisions. He is his own person. He acts his own

acts. I can agree with them or disagree with them. If I ever find them nauseous enough, I have a responsibility to leave and not deal with it any more.
Q: What about children?
A: I...I would say I have a legal responsibility for them, but in a sense I think they in turn are responsible for their own acts."

8. See André Comte-Sponville, *A Short Treatise on the Great Virtues: The Uses of Philosophy in Everyday Life*, translated by Catherine Temerson (London: William Heinemann, 2002) pp. 140-148.

9. If I were to put it in Levinas' terms, I would say that the self is called by that which is other than itself, it is commanded and consecrated by the face. Therefore the other is higher and more sublime than the self.

TWO: HOW THE COMA BEGAN

1. Although certain commentators claim that the fruit in question was the sexual act, others counter that this could not be true since God had commanded Adam and Eve to be fruitful and multiply even before they turned disobedient (see Genesis 1:28). Of course the latter argument makes the (reasonable) presumption that being fruitful and multiplying was intended from the beginning to occur by means of sexual intercourse.

2. In putting together my reflections on this primordial story, I have benefited from Eugen Drewermann's illuminating analysis of this encounter in *Strukturen des Bösen. Teil 1: Die jahwistische Urgeschichte in exegetischer Sicht* (Paderborn: Verlag Ferdinand Schöningh, 1977), especially pp. 55-67. However, I beg to read differently into the story in two crucial respects—the psychological interpretation based on anxiety that Drewermann upholds and his minimization of Eve's freedom. In fact, it is because of the importance he gives to anxiety in the whole chain of events that he cannot see any stage in this narration of Eve's temptation where she could have acted differently (See *ibid.*, p. 76).

3. Emmanuel Levinas, "Prayer Without Demand," in *The Levinas Reader*, edited by Seán Hand, (Oxford and Cambridge, Massachusetts: Basil Blackwell, 1989) p. 233.

4. *Ibid.*

THREE: FALSE HOPE

1. In fact his magnum opus *Totality and Infinity: An Essay on Exteriority*, translated by Alphonso Lingis (Pittsburgh: Duquesne University Press, 1969) begins with this arresting statement: "Everyone will agree that it is of the highest importance to know whether we are not duped by morality." (p. 21).

2. As Levinas puts it: "Being's interest takes dramatic form in egoisms struggling with one another, each against all." Emmanuel Levinas, *Otherwise than Being or Beyond Essence, op. cit.,* p. 4.

3. According to Levinas, the only way to peace is through demolishing the arrogant science of being where nothing is truly other but only relatively so, always ultimately reducible to the reassurance of sameness. Many prominent analysts of our culture are not as pessimistic regarding Western philosophy. In *The Great Disruption: Human Nature and the Reconstitution of the Social Order* (New York: The Free Press, 1999) Francis Fukuyama subscribes to an Aristotelian inspired view of human nature as essentially social, and that stresses the willingness of individuals to sacrifice their own claims for the sake of the wider social good. Therefore, despite the fact that the 1960s unleashed a wave of individualism that caused "great disruption" to the social order, Fukuyama predicts that we are on the brink of a new era, "the Great Reconstruction," which may successfully combine capitalism and communitarian values. However, for Levinas, this kind of thinking would still not be "radical" enough: that is, it does not get to the root [*radix*] of the problem. Levinas is not simply content with challenging the scope and extent of individual freedom. He wants to challenge the fact of individual freedom itself, which he believes to be essentially capricious and even violent by nature. According to him, it is only in measuring oneself against the idea of infinity that the fundamental injustice and unworthiness of one's freedom become apparent.

4. According to Levinas, philosophy needs to step outside of Occidental ontology, which is essentially warlike. In *Totality and Infinity* Levinas demands a paradigm shift, a move from totality to infinity, a shift to a new way of relation to being. Levinas suggests an eschatological relationship with it. By this he does not mean a relationship with being that occurs beyond history in a chronological and teleological sense. Rather he uses the term to indicate a relationship with being that occurs beyond the totality of history, beyond the sum of events that can be thought or conceptualized. "Eschatology institutes a relation with being *beyond the totality* or beyond history, and not with being beyond the past and the present." Emmanuel Levinas, *Totality and Infinity, op. cit.*, p. 22.

5. George Steiner, *Real Presences*, (Chicago: The University of Chicago Press, 1989) p. 143.

FOUR: SIGNS OF WAKEFULNESS

1. For more thoughts on this juxtaposition of their insignificance alongside their election by an omnipotent, transcendent deity, see Norman Cantor, *The Sacred Chain: A History of the Jews*, (London: HarperCollins Publishers, 1995), pp. 9-12.

2. Blaise Pascal, *Pensées*, translated with a revised introduction by A.J. Krailsheimer, (London: Penguin Books, 1995) p. 53.

3. Martin Buber, *I and Thou*, a new translation with a prologue "I and You" and notes by Walter Kaufmann, (Edinburgh: T. & T. Clark, 1970) p. 80. In a similar vein he writes: "In the beginning is the relation—as the category of being, as readiness, as a form that reaches out to be filled, as a model of the soul;

the *a priori* of relation; *the innate You.*" *Ibid.,* p. 78.

4. See Martin Buber, *Meetings*, edited with an introduction by Maurice Friedman, (La Salle, Illinois: Open Court Publishing Company, 1973).

5. "This parable portrays a spiritual pilgrimage from appearance to reality. We turn around, we climb up, we raise our heads. At each stage we see at first the *shadows* of what is more real and true." Iris Murdoch, *Metaphysics as a Guide to Morals*, (London: Chatto & Windus, 1992) p. 10.

6. "Man is only a reed, the weakest in nature, but he is a thinking reed. There is no need for the whole universe to take up arms to crush him: a vapor, a drop of water is enough to kill him. But even if the universe were to crush him, man would still be nobler than his slayer, because he knows that he is dying and the advantage the universe has over him. The universe knows none of this." Blaise Pascal, *Pensées, op. cit.,* p. 66.

7. *Ibid.,* p. 324.

8. See the chapter entitled "On Passing By" in Friedrich Nietzsche, *Thus Spoke Zarathustra*, translated by R.J. Hollingdale (London: Penguin Books, 1969), pp. 195-8.

9. See Abraham H. Maslow, *Motivation and Personality*, (New York: Harper, 1954).

FIVE: A SECULAR WAKE-UP CALL

1. All the short stories I will look at come from Raymond Carver's final collection, spanning stories from his entire life work, entitled *Where I'm Calling From: New and Selected Stories*, (New York: Vintage Contemporaries, 1989).

2. *Ibid.,* p. 43.

3. Emmanuel Levinas, "Ethics of the Infinite" in Richard Kearney, *States of Mind: Dialogues with Contemporary Thinkers on the European Mind* (Manchester: Manchester University Press, 1995) p. 192.

SIX: THE FACE THAT WAKES US UP

1. As opposed to Greek philosophy, which prioritizes vision, Jewish tradition highlights hearing, though without thereby discounting sight.

2. Hans Urs von Balthasar, *Spouse of the Word: Explorations in Theology II*, translated by A.V. Littledale with Alexander Dru, (San Francisco: Ignatius Press 1991) pp. 473-90.

3. *Ibid.,* p. 480.

4. *Ibid.,* p. 484.

5. See *Poems of Akhmatova*, selected, translated and introduced by Stanley Kunitz with Max Hayward (Boston and New York: Mariner Books, 1973), p. 99.

SEVEN: ALIVE OR COMATOSE—JOHN OR JUDAS?

1. John Paul II, *Crossing the Threshold of Hope,* edited by Vittorio Messori, translated by Jenny McPhee and Martha McPhee (London: Jonathan Cape, 1994), p. 186.

2. There has been an ongoing discussion among Kierkegaardian scholars regarding the relationship between Kierkegaard's own opinions and those expressed by his pseudonymous authors. Kierkegaard himself fired the debate by declaring peremptorily "So in the pseudonymous works there is not a single word that is mine, I have no opinion about these works except as a third person, no knowledge of their meaning except as a reader." *Concluding Unscientific Postscript to the Philosophical Fragments,* translated by David F. Swenson and Walter Lowrie (Princeton: Princeton University Press, 1968), p. 551. But this extreme claim needs to be tempered by the knowledge that many of the views expressed by his pseudonyms, especially by Johannes Climacus, are also articulated by Kierkegaard in his private journals. Furthermore, the above quotation neither states that Kierkegaard agrees or disagrees with the views of the pseudonymous authors: despite appearances, it leaves the matter open. In this sense, it is more an expression of distance than one of disagreement. Fundamentally, there seem to be two reasons for Kierkegaard's strong disclaimer. Firstly, he wants to force readers to engage with the views expressed in the pseudonymous works on their own merits rather than accepting them because Kierkegaard himself holds them or rather than using these views as simply a means of trying to understand the psychology of Kierkegaard himself. Secondly, the use of these invented pseudonyms allows Kierkegaard to present diverse perspectives on how to understand the world and exist in it, in order to help readers to become Christians—see Søren Kierkegaard, *The Point of View of My Work as an Author: A Report to History,* translated by Walter Lowrie, (New York: Harper Torchbooks, 1962) p. 13. It seems fair to conclude that Kierkegaard shared many of the views of the pseudonymous authors, but that caution must be used in identifying his opinions automatically or uncritically with theirs.

3. "The objective problem consists of an inquiry into the truth of Christianity. The subjective problem concerns the relationship of the individual to Christianity." Søren Kierkegaard, *Concluding Unscientific Postscript, op. cit.,* p. 20.

4. In this sense my position is not the either-or of Johannes Climacus, but the both-and of combining passionate interest and objective inquiry. Climacus paints the alternatives in stark brushstrokes: "The inquiring subject must be in one or the other of two situations. Either he is in faith assured of his own relationship to it, in which case he cannot be infinitely interested in all the rest, since faith itself is the infinite interest in Christianity, and since every other interest may readily come to constitute a temptation. Or, the inquirer is, on the other hand, not in an attitude of faith, but objectively in an attitude of contemplation, and hence not infinitely interested in the determination of the question."

Ibid., p. 23.

5. Some scholars see Judas in a much more sympathetic light. See for instance William Klassen, *Judas: Betrayer or Friend of Jesus?* (Minneapolis: Fortress Press, 1996).

6. Søren Kierkegaard, *The Sickness Unto Death,* translated with an introduction by Alastair Hannay (London: Penguin Classics, 1989) pp. 62-3.

EIGHT: WAKE UP, SLEEPING BEAUTY!

1. Pontopiddan wrote this short story as a riposte to Hans Christian Andersen's fairy tale, "The Ugly Duckling." He wanted to show that however liberating a person's sense of innate dignity may be, it is not strong enough to free them from an imprisoning cultural context. Pontoppidan is correct to the extent that we cannot realize ourselves independently of culture. But at the same time, we cannot simply allow ourselves to be the compliant slaves of a dehumanizing culture. We need to challenge and counter it.

2. "All these examples of wretchedness prove his greatness. It is the wretchedness of a great lord, the wretchedness of a dispossessed king." Blaise Pascal, *Pensées, op. cit.,* p. 29.

3. Hans Urs von Balthasar, *The Glory of the Lord: A Theological Aesthetics. Volume 1: Seeing the Form,* translated by Erasmo Leiva-Merikakis (Edinburgh: T. & T. Clark, 1982), p. 152.

4. Fyodor Dostoevsky, *The Idiot,* translated by Alan Myers, (Oxford: Oxford University Press, 1992) p. 148.

NINE: RESPONSIBILITY FOR ALL

1. Interestingly when Levinas was asked what led him to philosophy, he answered that it was most of all a result of reading Dostoevsky: "Je pense que ce sont d'abord mes lectures russes. C'est précisément Pouchkine, Lermontov et Dostoïevski, surtout Dostoïevski. Le roman russe, le roman de Dostoïevski et de Tolstoï, me paraissait très préoccupé des choses fondamentales. Livres traversés par l'inquiétude religieuse, mais lisible comme quête du sens de la vie." François Poirié, *Emmanuel Lévinas: Qui êtes-vous?* (Lyon: La Manufacture, 1987) p. 69. The influence of Russian authors such as Dostoevsky, Tolstoy Pushkin, and Lermontov upon Levinas has received scant attention in the secondary literature. A notable exception is Andrius Valevicius who, borrowing from many ideas in Nicolas Berdyaev's *The Russian Idea*—translated by R.M. French, (London: The Centenary Press, 1947)—gives a general account of the impact of Russian thought upon Levinas' philosophy in *From the Other to the Totally Other: The Religious Philosophy of Emmanuel Levinas,* (New York: Peter Lang Publishing, Inc., 1988) pp. 147-155.

2. "Biblical quotations or allusions were to Dostoevsky what the shaping background of myth had been to the Greek dramatists. The holy words, inex-

haustibly familiar and, until recent times, encrusted in the very fabric of the western and Russian mind, give the Dostoevskyan text its particular tonality." George Steiner, *Tolstoy or Dostoevsky: An Essay in Contrast*, (London: Faber and Faber, 1959) p. 301.

3. Fyodor Dostoevsky, *The Brothers Karamazov*, translated by Constance Garnett, revised by Ralph E. Matlaw, with backgrounds and sources and essays in criticism, (New York and London: W.W. Norton & Company, Inc., 1976) p. 298.

4. *Ibid.*, p. 65.

5. *Ibid.*, pp. 736-744.

6. *Ibid.*, pp. 738.

7. Levinas repeatedly quotes this decisive line from *The Brothers Karamazov* in his writings: "Each of us is guilty before everyone, for everyone and for everything, and I more than the others." Emmanuel Levinas, *Of God Who Comes to Mind*, translated by Bettina Bergo (Stanford: Stanford University Press, 1998), p. 72.

8. "When he [the monk] realizes that he is not only worse than others, but that he is responsible to all men for all and everything, for all human sins, general and individual, only then the aim of our seclusion is attained. For know, dear ones, that every one of us is undoubtedly responsible for all men and everything on earth, not merely through the general sinfulness of creation, but each one of us personally for all mankind and every individual man. This knowledge is the crown of life for the monk and for every man. For monks are not a special sort of men, but only what all men ought to be. Only through that knowledge, our heart grows soft with infinite, universal, inexhaustible love." Fyodor Dostoevsky, *The Brothers Karamazov, op. cit.*, p. 149.

9. *Ibid.*, p. 268.

10. *Ibid.*

11. *Ibid.*, p. 277.

12. *Ibid.*, p. 282.

13. Dostoevsky is drawing on the enormous breadth of Orthodox spirituality, which teaches a compassion that is literally cosmic in its dimensions. For instance the great Eastern saint, Isaac of Syria, recommended tears of love that could embrace all of creation: "The heart that is inflamed in this way embraces the entire creation—man, birds, animals, and even demons. At the recollection of them, and at the sight of them, such a man's eyes fill with tears that arise from the great compassion that presses on his heart. The heart grows tender and cannot endure to hear of or to look upon any injury or even the smallest suffering inflicted upon anything in creation. For this reason such a man prays increasingly with tears even for irrational animals and for the enemies of truth and for all who harm it, that they may be guarded and be forgiven." Quoted in Seely Beggiani, *Introduction to Eastern Spirituality: The Syriac Tradition*, (Montrose, Pennsylvania: Ridge Row Press, 1991) p. 75.

14. For an illuminating discussion of holy folly, see Hans Urs von Balthasar, *The Glory of the Lord: A Theological Aesthetics. Volume 5: The Realm of Metaphysics in the Modern Age,* translated by Oliver Davies et al. (Edinburgh: T. & T. Clark, 1991), pp. 141-204.

TEN: LIVING HUMILITY WITH HOPE IN HOLY WEEK

1. The Left Behind series of Christian fiction, for instance, which pushes a strongly evangelical and highly dramatic interpretation of world events, has already sold more than 50 million copies. It depicts a world speeding toward Armageddon. The eleventh novel in the Left Behind Series by Tim La Haye and Jerry B. Jenkins, entitled *Armageddon: The Cosmic Battle of the Ages* (Carol Stream, Illinois: Tyndale House Publishers, 2003), was released in April, 2003. The tenth novel in the series, *The Remnant: On the Brink of Armageddon* entered the *New York Times* Bestseller List at Number 1 when it was published. The previous novel in the Left Behind Series, *Desecration: Antichrist Takes The Throne,* also by Tim La Haye and Jerry B. Jenkins, was the bestselling hardback novel of 2001 in the USA.

2. Douglas Adams, *The Hitchhiker's Guide to the Galaxy* (New York, Ballantine Books, 1995), p. 156.

3. Inspired by the mystical experiences of Adrienne von Speyr, von Balthasar's theology of Holy Saturday insists upon the totally passive descent of the deceased Jesus not just into the place of the dead who are awaiting salvation, but as far as the hell of damnation itself, to the realm of those who have definitively separated themselves from God. I must admit that this vision von Balthasar conjures up of universal salvation through the utter solidarity of Jesus even with the damned casts a certain spell over me. But on sober reflection I am not sure whether von Balthasar's vision is excessive. I find it salutary to remind myself of a lucid insight of Wittgenstein: "Philosophy is a battle against the bewitchment of our intelligence by means of language." Ludwig Wittgenstein, *Philosophical Investigations,* translated by G.E.M. Anscombe (Oxford: Basil Blackwell, 1963) p. 47, § 109. Von Balthasar was a man of extraordinary culture who made an immense contribution to theology, but at times I wonder if his stirring rhetoric bewitches the mind through its sheer brilliance. In fact I also find that George Steiner's eloquent prose can exercise a similarly ambiguous fascination. For a brief presentation by von Balthasar of this imaginative approach to Holy Saturday, see *The Von Balthasar Reader,* edited by Medard Kehl and Werner Löser, translated by Robert Daly and Fred Lawrence (New York: Crossroad, 1982) pp. 150-3.

4. "A little kindness going only from man to man, not crossing distances to get to the places where events and forces unfold! A remarkable utopia of the good or the secret of its beyond." Emmanuel Levinas, *On Thinking-of-the-*

Other: Entre Nous, op. cit., p. 230.

5. Douglas Coupland, *Girlfriend in a Coma* (London: Flamingo, 1998).

6. Isabel Allende, *Paula*, translated by Margaret Sayers Peden (London: Flamingo, 1995).

7. In *The Story of Art* (London: Phaidon Press, 1989) p. 293, Ernst Gombrich mentions Holbein's "wonderful skill in the rendering of details" as one of his outstanding virtues as a painter.

8. Fyodor Dostoevsky, *The Idiot*, op. cit., 430.

9. See for instance John Rowlands' study *Holbein: The Paintings of Hans Holbein the Younger: complete edition* (Boston: David R. Godine, 1985).

Bibliography

Allende, Isabel. *Paula.*Translated by Margaret Sayers Peden. London: Flamingo, 1995.

von Balthasar, Hans Urs. *The Glory of the Lord: A Theological Aesthetics. Volume 1: Seeing the Form.* Translated by Erasmo Leiva-Merikakis. Edinburgh: T. & T Clark, 1982.

———. *Spouse of the Word: Explorations in Theology II.* Translated by A.V. Littledale with Alexander Dru. San Francisco: Ignatius Press, 1991.

Carver, Raymond. *Where I'm Calling From: New and Selected Stories.* New York: Vintage Contemporaries, 1989.

Comte-Sponville, André. *A Short Treatise on the Great Virtues: The Uses of Philosophy in Everyday Life.* Translated by CatherineTemerson. London: William Heinemann, 2002.

Coupland, Douglas. *Girlfriend in a Coma.* London: Flamingo, 1998.

Dostoevsky, Fyodor. *The Brothers Karamazov.* Translated by Constance Garnett, revised by Ralph E. Matlaw, with backgrounds and sources and essays in criticism. Norton Critical Edition. New York and London: W.W. Norton & Company, Inc., 1976.

Hand, Seán. *The Levinas Reader.* Oxford and Cambridge, Massachusetts: Basil Blackwell, 1989.

Kunitz, Stanley and Hayward, Max (Translation, editing and introduction). *Poems of Akhmatova.* Boston and New York: Mariner Books, 1973.

Lane, Robert E. *The Loss of Happiness in Market Democracies*. New Haven and London: Yale University Press, 2000.

Levinas, Emmanuel. *Ethics and Infinity, Conversations with Philippe Nemo*. Translated by Richard A. Cohen. Pittsburgh, Pennsylvania: Duquesne University Press, 1985.

———. *Totality and Infinity: An Essay on Exteriority*. Translated by Alphonso Lingis. Pittsburgh, Pennsylvania: Duquesne University Press, 1969.

Myers, David G. *The American Paradox: Spiritual Hunger in an Age of Plenty*. New Haven: Yale University Press, 2000.

Pascal, Blaise. *Pensées*. Translated with a revised introduction by A.J. Krailsheimer. London: Penguin Books, 1995.

Phillips, Adam. *Darwin's Worms*. London: Faber and Faber, 1999.

Putnam, Robert D. *Bowling Alone: The Collapse and Revival of American Community*. New York: Simon and Schuster, 2000.

Steiner, George. *Real Presences*. Chicago: The University of Chicago Press, 1989.

Index

Abraham, 65, 72, 73, 100, 115
Adam and Eve, 15, 22, 36–44,
  46, 73, 83, 85, 116, 133,
  139–41, 154, 195n
Adams, Douglas, 167, 201n
Akhmatova, Anna, 95, 106–7,
  197n
Allende, Isabel, 177–79, 202n
Aniston, Jennifer, 29
Aristotle, 80
Augustine of Hippo, 60, 71, 117
Bach, Johann Sebastian, 67
von Balthasar, Hans Urs, 14,
  98–100, 146, 168, 197n,
  199n, 201n
Barth, Karl, 61
Becker, Wolfgang, 176
Bellah, Robert, 25, 194–95n
Beckett, Samuel, 36
Bon Jovi, Jon, 28
Bono, 17
Buber, Martin, 76-77, 196–97n
Cain and Abel, 22, 60, 133
Carrey, Jim, 29
Catherine of Siena, Saint, 144
Carver, Raymond, 85, 86–91,
  92, 197n
Chesterton, G.K., 11
Comte–Sponville, André,
  30–31, 195n
Coupland, Douglas, 175, 202n
Dante Aligheri, 65, 169

Darwin, Charles, 19
Dickens, Charles, 17
Donne, John, 28
Dostoevsky, Fyodor, 14, 15,
  124, 139, 147, 148, 149–57,
  161, 183–4
Drewermann, Eugen, 195n
Eliot, T. S., 69, 97
Francis of Assisi, Saint, 161,
  162
Freeman, Morgan, 29
Freud, Sigmund, 19
Grant, Hugh, 28
Gray, John, 92
Heep, Uriah, 17
Holbein, Hans, 183–85, 201nn
Hopkins, Gerard Manley, 21
Homer, 65
Hornby, Nick, 28
Ignatius of Loyola, Saint, 13, 74
Jesus, 12, 13, 14, 15-16, 24,
  31–33, 39, 44, 48, 50, 52,
  62–63, 67–68, 69, 70–71,
  79–80, 81–84, 93–94, 100,
  101–6, 108, 109, 111–37,
  141, 147–48, 153–54, 156,
  157, 166, 168–70, 173,
  180–82, 183–87
John the Apostle, Saint, 14,
  15–16, 24, 31, 39, 79, 94, 98,
  101, 104, 109–26, 128–32,
  134–37, 143, 148, 153–55,

John the Apostle, Saint,
(continued)
  157, 167, 169–70, 173, 179,
  181, 184, 187
Judas Iscariot, 102, 109–10,
  115, 118–20, 122–33,
  136–37, 154, 170, 199n
Fukuyama, Francis, 196n
Kidman, Nicole, 92
Kierkegaard, Søren, 110, 144,
  172, 198–99n
Lane, Robert E., 194n
Larkin, Philip, 76
Lawrence of the Resurrection,
  68–69
Lazarus, 125–27, 129
Lennon, John, 27
Levinas, Emmanuel, 14–15, 23,
  14, 28–29, 44, 45, 53–56, 58,
  61–62, 65
Magi (Wise Men), 69
Mandela, Nelson, 27
Mary of Lazarus, 126–29, 153,
  169
Maslow, Abraham, 82, 197n
Marx, Karl, 72
Michelangelo, 134, 184
Mother Teresa of Calcutta, 27,
  92–93, 174
Myers, David G., 25, 193–94n
Nietzsche, Friedrich, 78, 80,
  197n
O'Connor, Flannery, 86
Parks, Rosa, 27
Pascal, Blaise, 56, 75, 78, 110,
  196–97n, 199n
Peter, Saint, 31–33, 113, 117,
  130, 132–33, 135, 166, 170,
  173, 185
Philippe, Marie-Dominique,
  193n
Phillips, Adam, 19–21, 193n
Plato, 52, 77

Pontoppidan, Henrik, 141, 199n
Pope John Paul II, 109, 198n
Putnam, Robert D., 25, 193n
Pythagoras, 22
Rahner, Karl, 61
Reeves, Keanu, 53
Rilke, Rainer Maria, 156
Sartre, Jean-Paul, 90–91
Satan, 36, 39, 73–74, 81–82,
  124, 131
Shakespeare, William, 55,
  95–96
Socrates, 77–78
Stalin, Josef, 107
Steiner, George, 60, 165, 168,
  196n, 199n
Tolkien, J.R.R., 27, 30
Thérèse of Lisieux, Saint,
  189–91
Ulysses, 65
Virgin Mary, 47, 70–71, 72–73,
  114, 121, 134, 170, 186
Wiesel, Elie, 45
Wittgenstein, Ludwig, 201n
Yeats, William Butler, 144, 176